W9-BXT-563

HONOR GIRL

Maggie Thrash

CANDLEWICK PRESS

LOOK, DREW, YOUR SISTER FOUND A TUMBLEWEED!

I'M INTENSELY PROUD.

SMILE!

NEW MEXICO, 17 YEARS OLD

It's November. We're here visiting my brother at St. John's College.
BOOK OF THE NEW SUN

I DON'T APPROVE OF YOU RUNNING OFF WITH THIS PERSON YOU HAVEN'T SEEN IN TWO YEARS.
YOUR BROTHER WILL THINK YOU DON'T CARE ABOUT HIM.
BOOK OF THE NEW SUN

DREW, DO YOU MIND IF I SPEND A FEW HOURS WITH MY FRIEND?

I'M BITTERLY RESENTFUL.
BOOK OF THE NEW SUN

SEE!

THAT'S HER.
THAT'S SHE.
HEY.
HEY . . .
UM, WE GOT YOU THIS.
THANK YOU!

THIS IS MY MOM AND MY BROTHER.
IT'S NICE TO MEET YOU. . . .

SO WHAT DO YOU GIRLS PLAN TO DO TODAY?
I THOUGHT WE'D DRIVE TO THE PUYE CLIFFS. IF THAT'S OK.

HOW NICE! DREW, YOU SHOULD JOIN THEM!

. . .

DON'T YOU
DARE

GOSH. IF ONLY I WEREN'T SO . . . BUSY.

WELL . . . TOODLE-LOO, THEN.

BYE . . .

CAN I TELL YOU SOMETHING A LITTLE STRANGE?
SURE.

I NEVER EXPECTED TO SEE YOU AGAIN.
COLORADO

CHAPTER 1
Kentucky,
15 years old
I went to the same camp every year, one of the oldest camps in the South. It was deep in the mountains and so isolated that you had to cross a river on a man-pushed barge to get there. My mom went there, and her mom went there, and nothing had changed since 1922.

100-year-old barge

100-year-old tents

There were mandatory Civil War reenactments every morning.
BLUE!
GRAY!

It was literally the blues screaming "blue" and the grays screaming "gray" for twenty minutes.
BLUE!
GRAY!

I had a pillow with all my merit patches sewn on it.

most enthusiastic 1995
B
most improved
swim champ
legacy
tree hugger
BOOKWORM
spirit of DRAMA
1994
1995
1996
1997
1998
1999

I also had a leash I was supposed to wear at night to prevent sleepwalking, a problem I'd had since I was five.

Somnambu-Leash!
with Comfort Flex
YOU'RE NOT GOING ANYWHERE!
Zzzz

Everyone had to wear a uniform. My school had a uniform too, so I was used to it. I was used to environments where it was important for everyone to be the same.

There was very little diversity among the one hundred campers. Even the one Jewish girl had blond hair and blue eyes. Her name was Lexi, and every year she set the trends, like what to put in your hair and the right kind of socks and rolling the waistband of your shorts to make them shorter.

Most of the other girls were from Kentucky. They lived in the same towns as one another or went to the same boarding schools. I was the only girl from Atlanta.
CAMP BELLFLOWER
GREENBRIAR
APPALACHIAN
OZARKS
ATLANTA

Which meant I could be a completely different person if I wanted to.
swim champ
1996
1997
1998
1999
M. THRASH

FLAG LOWERING, 5:45 PM

This was my friend Shannon.
She was always aggravated by the younger campers.

I WISH THERE WERE AN INVISIBLE FENCE AROUND JUNIOR CAMP.

WE SHOULD PRETEND TO BE WITCHES AND SCARE THEM AWAY.
DO IT.

BEGONE, ODIOUS JUNIORS! OR I'LL COOK YER GIZZARDS!

AW, YOU MADE THEM CRY!
WHACK

CHILDREN, I WAS ONLY JOKING.

AAAAAA

UGH, THEY'RE RUNNING TO THEIR COUNSELOR.
NOW I'LL GET IN TROUBLE.
IT'S JUST ERIN.
SHE'LL BE COOL ABOUT IT.

This was Erin.

SORRY!
THOSE POOR CHILDREN.

COME ON, LET'S GO TO DINNER.

I knew Erin, but only because the same girls came to camp every year. I knew she was 19 and that she played guitar.
I don't think she knew anything about me.

HEY MAG, DID Y'ALL TAKE THE SEX POLL?

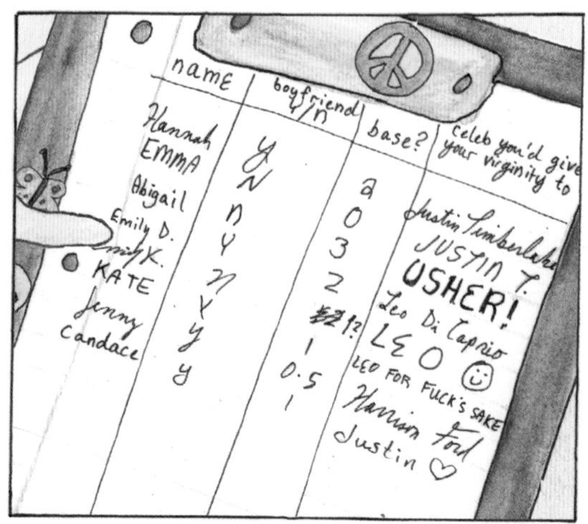
name
boyfriend Y/N
base?
Celeb you'd give your virginity to
Hannah
EMMA
Abigail
Emily D.
KATE
Jenny
Candace
Y
N
N
Y
N
Y
Y
Y
a
0
3
2
1
0.5
1
Justin Timberlake
JUSTIN T.
USHER!
Leo Di Caprio
LEO
LEO FOR FUCK'S SAKE
Harrison Ford
Justin

Harrison
Justin
Kevin

WHO'S KEVIN? KEVIN BACON?
NO.

KEVIN RICHARDSON.
OOOKAY.

Kevin Richardson was my favorite Backstreet Boy. I loved him because he seemed soulful and brooding, and he wore dark, billowing trench coats. You couldn't find boys like that in the South. At least not in my school.

GIRLS, IS THAT THE SEX POLL THAT'S BEEN FLOATING AROUND?
UM . . .
Tammy, head counselor

COME ON, USE YOUR HEADS.
WE HAVE EIGHT-YEAR-OLDS HERE.

WELCOME TO CAMP, YOUNG LADIES.
NO CANDY IN THE TENTS. OR WE'LL BE INFESTED WITH RATS AND VARMINTS.
Our camp director was an old man who came out occasionally to threaten us with a canoe paddle.

AND I'LL PADDLE YER BREECHES!

He was ancient and couldn't tell any of us apart. If you ever got in trouble, he'd probably call the wrong set of parents. But that was a moot point anyway, because no one ever broke the rules.
HAVE A NICE SUMMER, GLADYS.
OKEY-DOKE.

There was a 50-cent Coke machine behind the canoeing shed, strictly for counselors. Everyone knew it was there, and every day presented a hundred opportunities to slip behind the shed and sneak a wonderful, refreshing can of Coke. But I never knew a single girl who ever did, including me. That's just not who we were.

Who we were was a bunch of Christian girls who sang songs together. On the first night, we always serenaded the Honor Girl, a 16-year-old camper appointed the previous summer. The criteria for Honor Girl were vague, with no particular definition. It was just the one who seemed, in an unmistakable way, to represent the best of us. Everyone would light a candle, and at the end of the song, we'd each touch our flame to hers. It was meant to be symbolic — the Honor Girl imbuing us with her perfect spirit.

NOW I'M SCARED! I DON'T WANNA BE IN THE THRALL OF HORROR GIRL!
DON'T FIGHT IT, MAGGIE. TOUCH THE FLAME!

WINCE

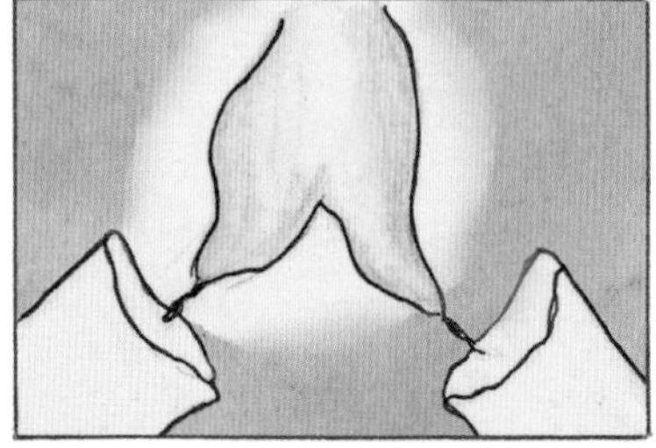

FEEL ANY DIFFERENT?
. . . NOPE. PRETTY MUCH THE SAME.

In senior camp we were on our own, with no counselors. We lived by the honor system. It wasn't really that they trusted us to be particularly responsible; they just trusted us to be obedient, even when no one was watching.
Harry Potter
ARE YOU WEARING YOUR FOOT LEASH?
my tent-mate Mary Kelly, who acted like everyone's mother
I DON'T WANT TO. IT'S ITCHY AND IT MAKES MY ANKLE SWEATY.
BUT YOU'LL WANDER OFF AND BE DEVOURED BY A BIG BLACK BEAR!
BLACK BEARS ARE HARMLESS, MARY KELLY. THEY DEVOUR DANDELIONS.
ABIGAIL, HOLD HER DOWN.
puppies for peace!
YANK
my other tent-mate Abigail, the most hyper girl in camp
WEAR YOUR FOOT LEASH, YOU BAD GIRL!
. . . GIRLS?
WHY IS YOUR TENT-MATE BEING CHAINED TO THE BED?

SHE IS A PRISONER OF TENT 2!
A SEXUAL PRISONER!
UH-HUH.
JUST KIDDING!

SO . . .

IT'S FOR SLEEPWALKING.

OK, I GOTTA SEE THIS.

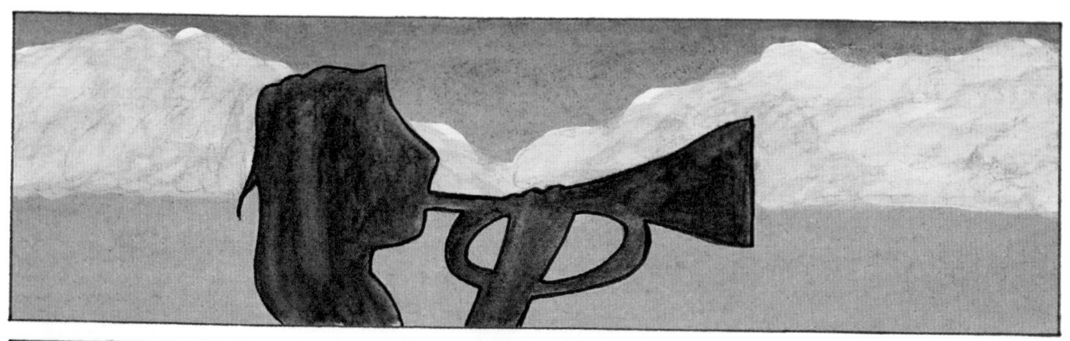

TAPS ALREADY?
puppies for peace!
WE HAVEN'T BRUSHED OUR TEETH YET!

GO AHEAD. JUST BE BACK IN FIVE MINUTES.
MAKE SURE MAGGIE KEEPS HER LEASH ON. SHE'S SO BAD!

I'LL WATCH HER. NOW, BE QUICK!

SO.

WAIT, WHAT AM I DOING HERE?

OH, YEAH! I CAME TO GIVE YOU THIS.
MY CAMPERS MADE IT FOR YOU.

Maggie

. . . GOSH.
WAIT, AM I . . . A PSYCHOTIC BIRTHDAY GIRL?

I THINK IT'S A WITCH'S HAT. THEY FORGOT TO DRAW THE BRIM.
AH, OF COURSE.

SO, SLEEPWALKING . . . THAT'S SO COOL.

IS IT?
I ALWAYS BUMP INTO STUFF AND WAKE EVERYONE UP.

IT'S DEFINITELY COOL.
IT'S LIKE . . . THE NIGHT IS CALLING TO YOUR SPIRIT.

BUT . . .

IT'S PROBABLY SAFER NOT TO ANSWER.

WELL, I BETTER GET BACK TO JUNIOR CAMP.
SEE YA!

'NIGHT.

CHAPTER 2
Ours Is the Boy Band of Dignity
est. 1922
Come to
Camp Bellflower
NO BOYS ALLOWED
smiling faces!
LEADERSHIP!
sportsmanship!
one word: WOW!
"It gets a little crazy!"
everyone can shine!
"TRADITION IS IMPORTANT"
BLUE
GRAY

WHY ARE THEY ADVERTISING CAMP TO US?
YEAH, WE'RE ALREADY HERE. IT'S NOT LIKE WE CAN LEAVE.

IT'S KIND OF MISLEADING, TOO.
HOW SO?

CAMP IS WAY MORE BORING THAN THAT.

IN A GOOD WAY.

HEY, CHICKADEES.
HI, MARY KELLY.

JILL'S LOOKING FOR YOU. I THINK SHE WANTS TO BE YOUR CANOEING PARTNER.
OH GOD.

MAAAAAAGGIEEE!

LET'S FUCKING ROW!

CHRIST, JILL. AREN'T YOU LIKE TEN YEARS OLD?

Every year I did canoeing because my mom did canoeing and her mom did canoeing. The boats were divvied up by height, and I was too short to row with anyone my own age. It never used to bother me, but now suddenly it really did.

ACTUALLY I'M NOT DOING CANOEING THIS YEAR.

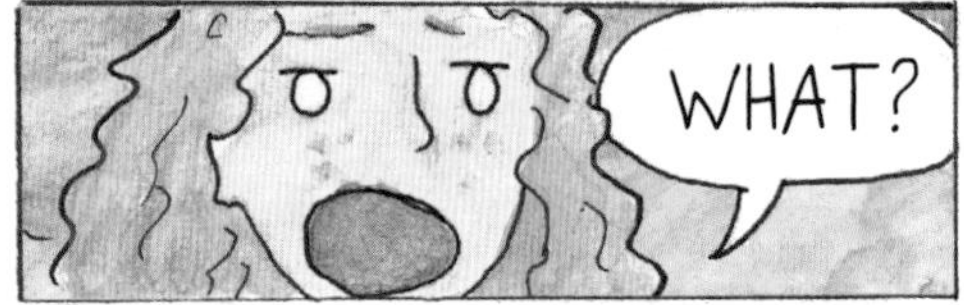
WHAT?

MAGGIE, YOU SHOULD DO DRAMA WITH ME.
MAYBE . . . WHAT'S THE PLAY?

Southern Fried
CRACKER TALES
a stage play
watermelon-size smiles!

I'LL THINK ABOUT IT.
WE'LL HAVE A REAL BARREL!

SHANNON, WHAT ARE YOU TAKING?
SOCCER, LACROSSE, FIELD HOCKEY . . .

YOU'RE SUCH A JOCK, SHANNON. LET ME FEEL YOUR ARM.
THE BRAIN IS THE STRONGEST MUSCLE.

IS IT REALLY?
MINE IS.

WHERE ARE YOU OFF TO?
THE RANGE. WHERE A GUN IS THE STRONGEST MUSCLE.
SEE YA.

The rifle range was the highest point in camp. It was such a hike that plenty of girls never even went there. That's part of why I liked it. I also liked the smell of gun smoke and bore solvent, and the hundred years' worth of brass bullet shells covering the ground. And the way the crack of every shot echoed down the hill.
WHAT ARE YOU DOING HERE?
This was Libby, the top shooter in camp.
JUST . . . SHOOTING, SAME AS YOU.

OH, OK . . .
WELL, I JUST . . .
I GUESS I THOUGHT I HAD THE RANGE TO MYSELF.

WELL, NOW **WE** HAVE IT TO **OUR**SELVES.

. . . GREAT.

Libby and I were both shooting for our Distinguished Expert certification, the highest award offered by the National Rifle Association. She was way better than me and had only 10 targets left. I had 33.

HOW'S LIFE ON THE RANGE?
PRETTY HILARIOUS. MAGGIE JUST MISSED THE TARGET.
CLAP CLAP

WHAT IS SHE EVEN DOING HERE THIS EARLY?
GOD, WHO KNOWS? JUST TAKING UP SPACE, APPARENTLY.

WELL, IT CAN'T BE THAT MUCH SPACE. SHE'S PRACTICALLY A MIDGET.

Is it a gun or a tree?
I can't tell!

YOU GOING TO SHOOT THAT THING OR WHAT?

IT'S RAINING.

Whenever it rained, we were immediately herded to the play hall, where the counselors would come up with some extravaganza to keep us from getting depressed. Usually it was a variant on the talent show, with a theme like Memorable TV Commercials or Disco-Rama: Hits of the '70s.

WE'LL TAKE BACKSTREET BOYS.
SHOVE

WELL, THERE'S A LINE.
AND BETHANY'S TENT ALREADY CALLED BACKSTREET BOYS.

WHICH BETHANY? TENNIS BETHANY OR BIG-FOOT BETHANY?
TENNIS BETHANY.

SO YOU CAN EITHER JOIN HER TENT OR YOU COULD TAKE . . .

O-Town was the lamest boy band in the history of boy bands. Their only hit was called "My Liquid Dreams," and it was the stupidest song ever. Not a single member of O-Town approached the hotness or soulfulness of Kevin Richardson.

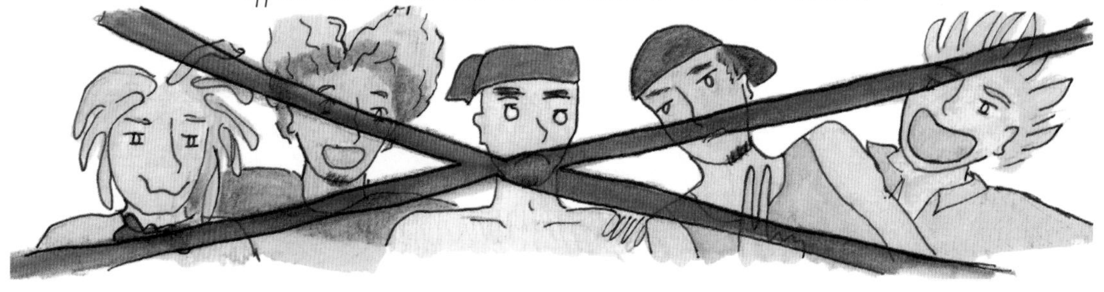

Tennis Bethany wasn't someone I'd hung out with before. She was younger than me, 14, and the different age groups didn't mix too much. I knew she was a National Junior tennis champion, and that she went to a weird Quaker school where all the teachers were hippies.

HEY!
HEY, BETHANY, CAN I DO BSB WITH Y'ALL?

SURE!
WE ALREADY HAVE A FANTASTIC PLAN!

BACKSTREET BUTTS! GET IT?!
WE'RE GONNA **MOON** EVERYONE ONSTAGE!

WHOA WHOA WHOA.
Gwen

YOU'RE NOT TAKING THIS SERIOUSLY.

HERE, SOMEONE GIVE ME A MARKER.

WATCH THIS.

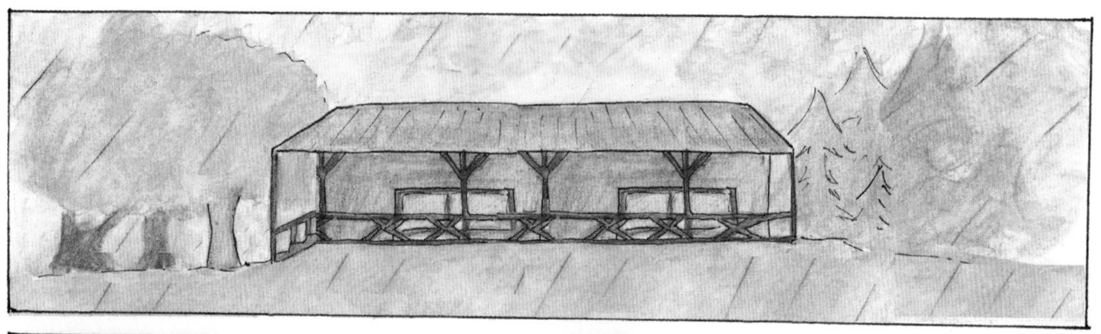

HEY, THEY STOLE OUR IDEA!
MMMBUTTS! GET IT?!

THEY CAN HAVE IT. OURS IS THE BOY BAND OF DIGNITY.

WHAT IF EVERYONE LAUGHS AT US?

RELAX, EVERYONE'S LAUGHING AT EVERYONE.

BUT IT'S DIFFERENT. THEY'RE LAUGHING AT THEIR BUTTS.
THEY'LL BE LAUGHING AT OUR FACES.

JUST PRETEND YOUR FACE **IS** YOUR BUTT!
I'M NOT DOING THIS. WE'RE GONNA LOOK STUPID.

FINE — GO, THEN.
WE DON'T NEED YOU.

READY?
I GUESS. . . .

You are my fire
The one desire

Believe...

when I say

I WANT IT THAT WAY

WHO IS THAT?

A BACKSTREET BOY, DUH. PROBABLY KEVIN.

NO, I MEAN . . .
WHO IS SHE?

THAT'S MAGGIE THRASH.

HEY!
YOU WERE TOTALLY AWESOME UP THERE!

WILL YOU SIGN MY CD?

Kevin
millennium
SURE.

KEVIN? NO, I WANT **YOU** TO SIGN IT.
OH . . . OK!

Kevin
MAGGIE
millennium

CHAPTER 3
Lice Scare

LUNCH, 1:00 PM
VOILÀ.
MERCI.
READ FAST — THERE'S A WAIT-LIST.
OKEY-DOKE.
OH MY GOD, LOOK.
I SAW HIM TAKE HIS SHIRT OFF ONCE.
REALLY?
HE HAS A SIX-PACK.
SO, MAGGIE, WHO'S YOUR FAVORITE SLOG BOY?

THE SLOG BOYS

These were the only boys in camp. Everyone had a favorite. We were supposed to leave them alone and let them do their jobs in peace, but they always became a point of obsession.

If you ever expressed any interest in a boy, especially a Slog Boy, the entire camp would burst into song. It happened at least once a day.

ABIGAIL, ABIGAIL

ABIGAIL'S IN LOVE!

WE KNOW HER HEART FLUTTERS
I WISH DANNY WEREN'T SO CUTE.

JUST LIKE A DOVE!
WE'RE GONNA HEAR THIS SONG A BILLION TIMES.

ABIGAIL, ABIGAIL
WELL, WE CAN ALL GO INSANE TOGETHER.
CLINK!

ABIGAIL LOVES DANNY!

REST HOUR, 2-3 PM
LADY JOCK

HEY MAGGIE, TELL ME WHAT YOU THINK.

Dear Danny
Your eyes are the stars and the stars are your eyes
That I love you should come as no surprise!
I hope you liked that poem! Sometimes I can be a little cheesey!!!!
= me
your ~~secret~~ admirer
Abigail

VERY NICE.

YAY! NOW LET'S GO PUT IT IN THE GARBAGE!

SMOOCH!

Danny

NOW WE NEED TO DO A CHANT.

CUPID, CUPID, COME TO US!

ALL RIGHT, WHAT TIME IS IT?
2:25.

PERFECT. WE CAN HIDE BEHIND THAT BUSH.

COME ON, Y'ALL. GET DOWN!

IS THAT TAMMY? WHAT'S SHE DOING?

LOOKS LIKE SOMEONE'S CANDY STASH GOT CONFISCATED.

SHE'S DUMPING IT ON MY LETTER!

I HAVE TO SAVE IT BEFORE DANNY GETS HERE!

JUST LEAVE IT, ABIGAIL! THE TRUCK'S COMING!

WHOA.

DIGGING CANDY OUT OF THE TRASH?
YOU MUST BE PRETTY DESPERATE.

STAY OFF THE CRACK!

WHAT IS SHE SO UPSET ABOUT?

DANNY'S LIKE TWENTY YEARS OLD. I'M SURE HE'S NOT INTERESTED IN CAMPERS.

DON'T SQUASH HER FANTASY, SHANNON.

I CAN HEAR YOU. AND I'M NOT SQUASHED.
I'M JUST IRRITATED BECAUSE I'M ALL ITCHY.

ITCHY LIKE . . . SEXUALLY?
UGH, NO, THE NORMAL KIND!

Y'ALL ARE **SO** IMMATURE!

Evening on the range

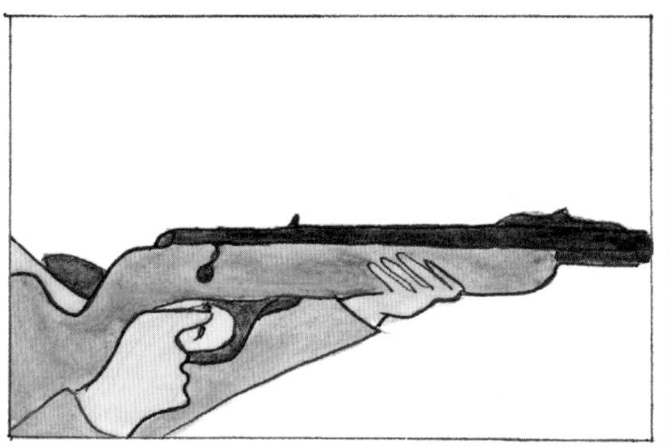

LIBBY, TERRIFICO.
MAGGIE . . . UM . . .

CAN YOU GIVE US A MINUTE, LIBBY? GO SHOOT IN THE OTHER STALL.

IT SMELLS LIKE SKUNK OVER THERE.

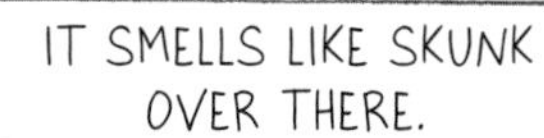
LIBBY, JUST DO IT.

FINE.

MAGGIE, COME LOOK AT THIS.

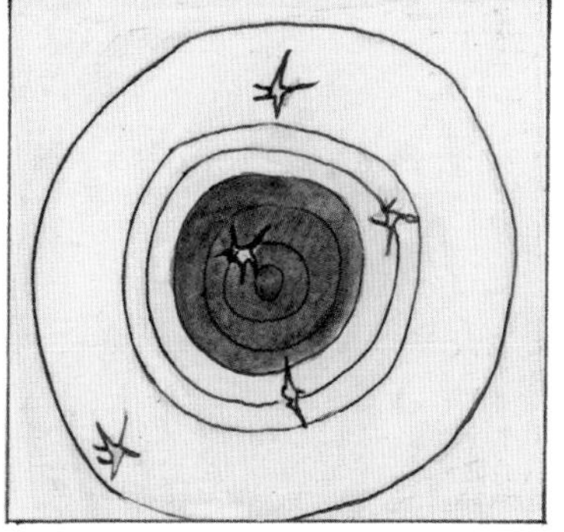

I KNOW I'M THE WORST, NICKY.

YEAH, I KNOW YOU KNOW YOU'RE THE WORST. THAT'S **WHY** YOU'RE THE WORST.

I MEAN, GET OUT OF YOUR HEAD. GIVE YOURSELF A FREAKING CHANCE.

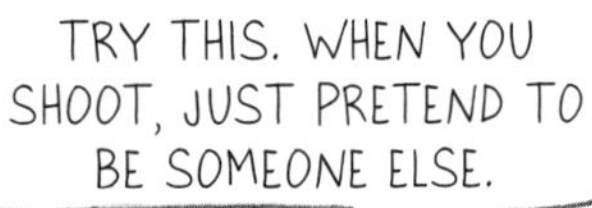
TRY THIS. WHEN YOU SHOOT, JUST PRETEND TO BE SOMEONE ELSE.

LIKE WHO?

LIKE ANNIE OAKLEY OR A CIA SNIPER. SOMEONE WHO WOULD NEVER MISS.

Straight through my heart
a single bullet got me

BANG

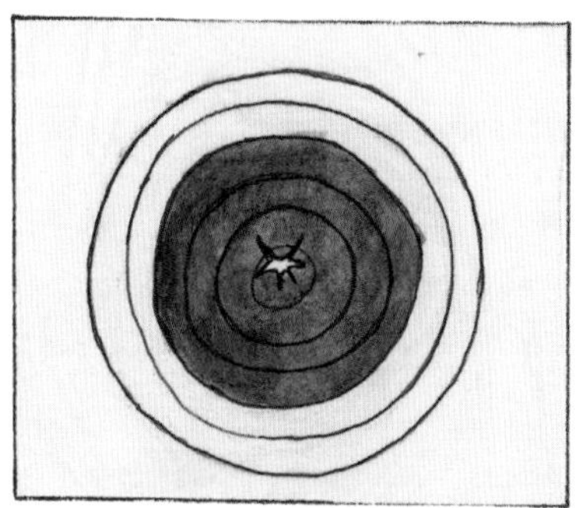

NICE. DO THAT AGAIN.

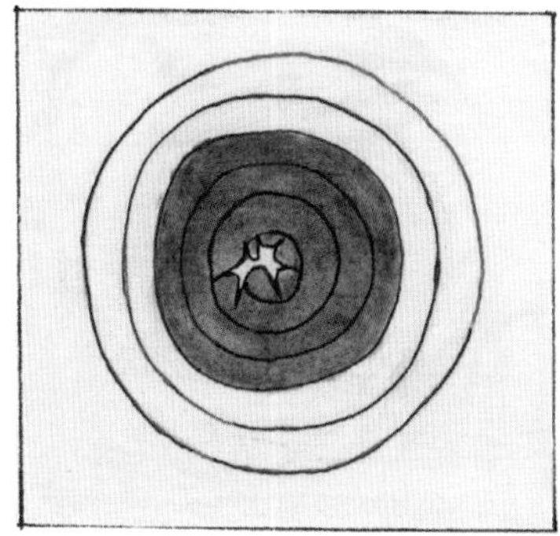

HEY, THAT'S A ONE-HOLE-GROUP!

BANG

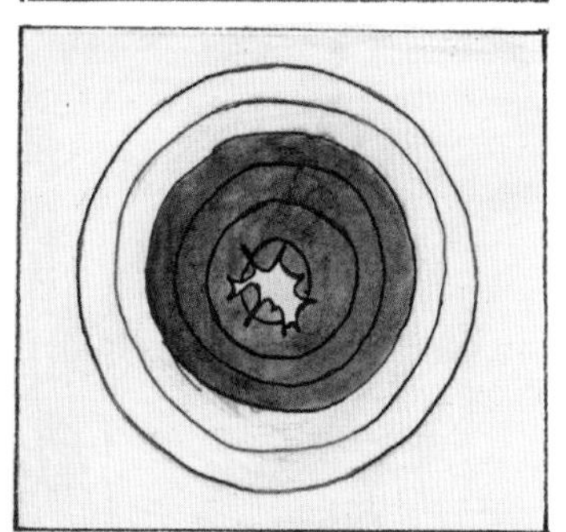

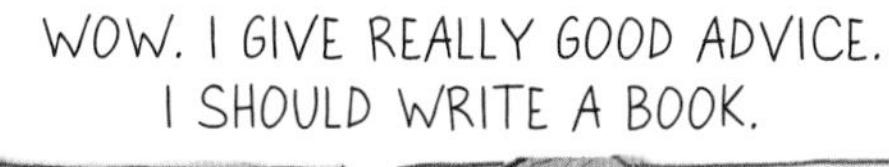
WOW. I GIVE REALLY GOOD ADVICE.
I SHOULD WRITE A BOOK.

CALL IT *NICKY'S TRICKIES!*

. . . NO.

KNOCK, KNOCK. I'M HERE TO FETCH MAGGIE. OUR UNIT'S BEING LICE-CHECKED.

NO WAY! MAGGIE CAN'T LEAVE NOW. SHE'S ON FIRE.

I'LL COME RIGHT BACK.
YOU BETTER.

ABIGAIL'S PSYCHOSOMATIC ITCHINESS HAS EVERYONE IN A PANIC.
YOU ARE SO LUCKY THAT REDHEADS NEVER GET LICE.

WHO TOLD YOU THAT?
YOU DID! LAST YEAR!

WOW. I WAS TOTALLY LYING.

LOOKS GOOD. YOU'RE CLEAR.

FELICEITATIONS.
HEH.

SO LONG, SUCKERS.
NEXT.

HEY ERIN.
OH, HEY! SIT ON DOWN.

YOU HAVE PRETTY HAIR.
THANK YOU.
IT'S LIKE A COCKER SPANIEL.

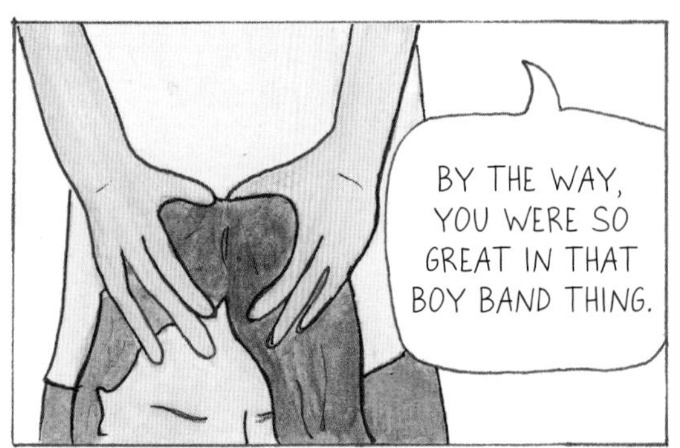
BY THE WAY, YOU WERE SO GREAT IN THAT BOY BAND THING.

YES. I MEAN . . . WHAT?

THE BACKSTREET BROTHERS. OR HANSON.
WHICHEVER ONE WAS YOU.

YOU'RE LICE-FREE.
GIVE THIS TO YOUR UNIT HEAD.
LICE ARE CRAAAAZY!
GET YOUR HEAD EXAMINED!
camper Maggie
inspector Erin

WHAT ARE YOU DOING?

NOTHING!

THEN WHY AREN'T YOU ON THE RANGE? I WAS WAITING FOR YOU, GIRL.
SORRY, I FORGOT.

WHAT'S THE MATTER? ARE YOU HAVING AN IDENTITY CRISIS?

WHAT?

WELL, ONE DAY YOU'RE JUST SOME GOOFY LOSER —
EXCUSE ME?
AND THE NEXT DAY YOU'RE SHOOTING ONE-HOLE-GROUPS LIKE A STAR.

BUT MAYBE YOU'D RATHER STAY A LOSER.
LOSERS GET TO CHILL WHILE THE WINNERS DUKE IT OUT.

SO IF YOU'D RATHER **CHILL** THAN BE A WINNER —
NICKY, FINE, I'LL BE A WINNER.
GOOD! GLAD IT'S DECIDED.

HEY, CAN I ASK YOU SOMETHING?
SURE.

HAVE YOU EVER HEARD OF A GAY CODE INVOLVING DOG BREEDS?
WHAT'S A GAY CODE?

YOU KNOW, LIKE A COVERT WAY FOR GAYS TO IDENTIFY EACH OTHER.
INVOLVING DOG BREEDS?

LIKE, MAYBE "COCKER SPANIEL" MEANS GAY, OR "BASSET HOUND" MEANS . . . NOT.

IF I WERE GAY, I'D JUST BARK AT EVERYONE.
DOES THAT ANSWER IT?

. . . I GUESS.
GREAT! THEN I'LL SEE YOU TOMORROW AT THE RANGE.
SLAP

STAY OUTTA YOUR HEAD, MAG.
OK.

MAGGIE.
HOW DARE YOU STARE INTO SPACE.

HMM?

YOU KNOW I'M NEXT ON THE WAIT-LIST.

READ LIKE THE WIND!

HERE, YOU CAN HAVE IT.
REALLY?

JUST TELL ME HOW IT ENDS.

YELLOW!

EW, DON'T GET YOUR LICE ON US.

OH, IT WAS JUST DANDRUFF. ISN'T THAT FUNNY?
HYSTERICAL.

MAGGIE, WHY ARE YOU SO MOPEY ALL OF A SUDDEN?

SHE ALWAYS GETS MOPEY AT FOOT-LEASH TIME.

BE GOOD, LITTLE MAGGIE.

TAPS, GALS. EVERYONE IN THEIR OWN BEDS, PLEASE.

YES, TAMMY.

I stayed up half the night trying to remember everything I could about her and every interaction we'd ever had.

- she's a vegetarian
- she has that weird guitar (a lute?)
- when I was 12 she won Honor Girl and the archery award, we were on the barge together, on the last day. I think I said congratulations
- I stood next to her at candlelight campfire... I think that was her?

GRAY!
GRAY!

GRAY!

INSPECTION

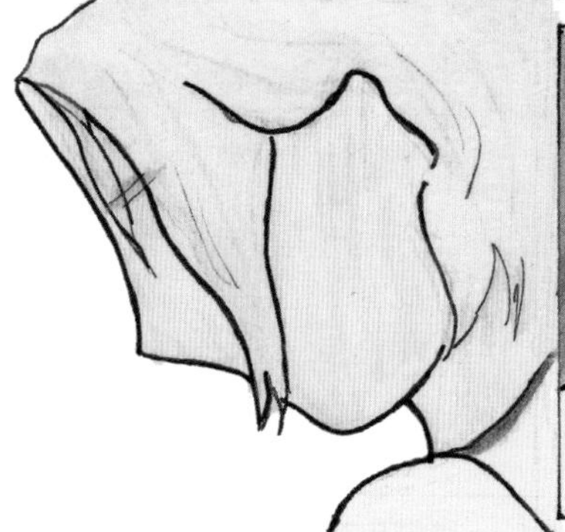

HEY.
DESERTER.

BACK TO THE CONFEDERATE LINE, PLEASE.

GRAY!

HUH? WHAT?

I SAID, I HEARD YOU SHOT A ONE-HOLE-GROUP.
YEAH.

WELL CONGRATS. EVERYONE DESERVES TO GET LUCKY ONCE.
THANKS. . . .

The twenty minutes of screaming always ended with a song about sportsmanship and everyone hugging each other.
RIVALS EVER MORE
FRIENDSHIP EVER SURE

HEY! WHY ARE YOU RUNNING?
BECAUSE IT'S FASTER THAN WALKING.

MAG! READY TO BLOW MY MIND?
YES.

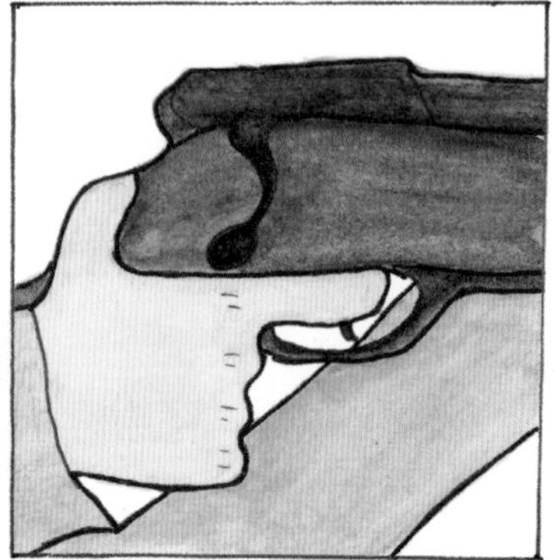

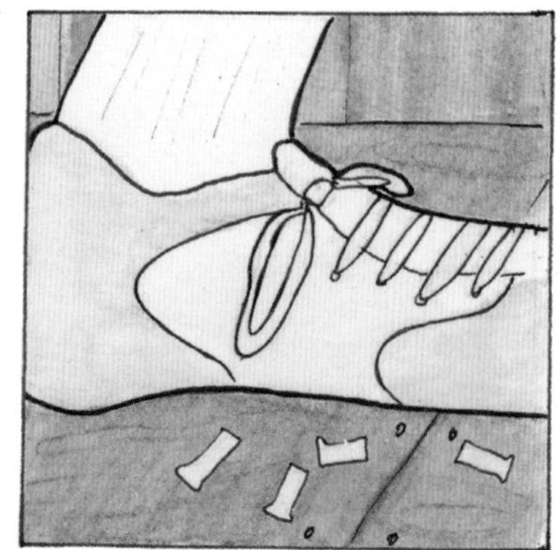

LIBBY, CHECK THIS OUT. MAGGIE'S BEEN REBORN.

BUT THAT'S NOT ALL FIVE SHOTS, IS IT?

1, 2, 3, 4, 5.

HUH, NICE JOB.
THANKS.

I used to take full seconds to steady my arm and aim before pulling the trigger. Now I just hoisted the gun and lined up the sights in a single motion, taking the shot the instant my eye glimpsed the center of the bull.

It only worked if I kept my mind completely blank.

Shooting perfect targets wasn't even the best part. The best part was that while I did it, I didn't have to think about Erin. I could come up for air, and just shoot and shoot and shoot.

CHAPTER 4
Freaks

helping hands
CHORES
litter patrol . . . Abigail
mail call . . . . . Ann C.
silverware . . . . . Maggie
bug juice . . . . . Mary Kelly
tabletops . . . . . Shannon

SILVERWARE? I THOUGHT I ASKED FOR MAIL CALL.
OH, I SWITCHED YOU!
WHY?
CHORES
FUN

SO YOU COULD BE WITH LUKE!
YOU'RE WELCOME, LOVER GIRL!
JAB

WARSH 'R GIT DRY THAR FARKS 'N SPWANS, Y'HAR?
. . . UH-HUH.

MAGGIE, HEY!

HI!

SILVERWARE, HUH? THAT'S THE WORST.

OH, IT'S NOT THAT BAD. THE SOAP IS TROPICAL SMELLING.

SO IT'S LIKE A BREAK FROM THE NORMAL SMELLS . . .

YOU KNOW, LIKE TREES . . . AND THE SKY.
SURE. GIVE YOUR NOSE A BREATHER.

WELL, I JUST STOPPED TO SAY HI, SO . . .
BYE.

BYE.

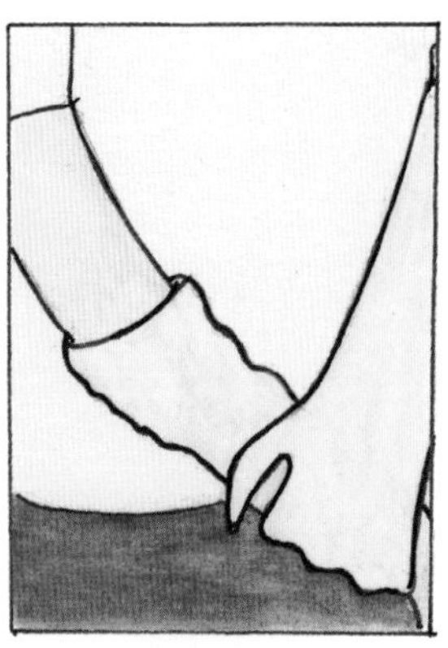

YANK

ERIN. WAIT.

YEAH?
UM, COULD YOU . . . PULL MY HAIR OUT OF MY FACE?
REAL QUICK?

. . . SURE.

DO YOU EVER WEAR A BRAID?

I ALWAYS JUST DO THE SAME THING.
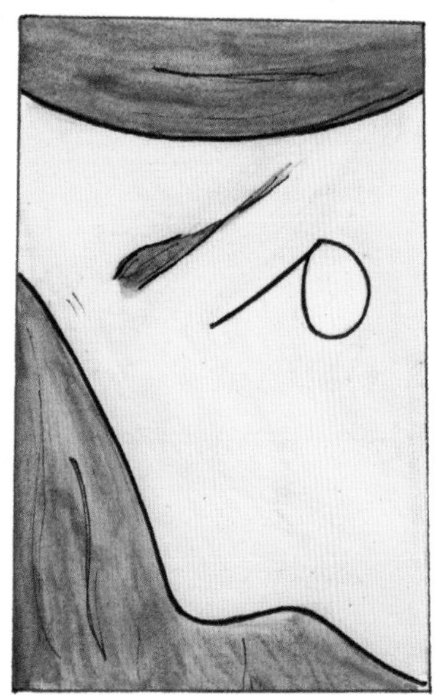

The second she touched me, I wanted to run. I couldn't believe how perverted I was being. You don't trick someone into touching you — not unless you're a creep or a molester.

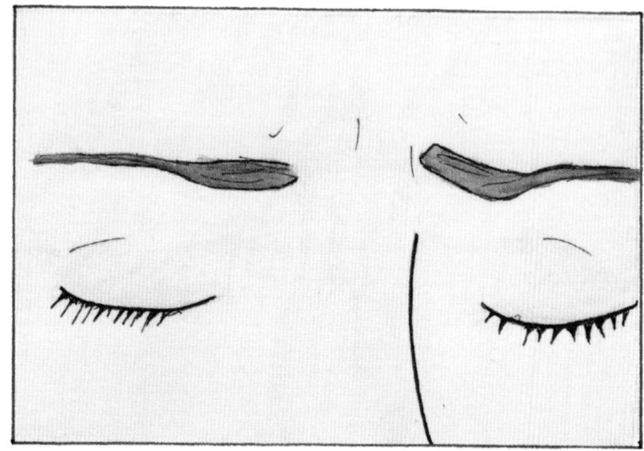

I could tell I was standing too still and breathing too silently. I prayed she didn't notice, but she must have, she was so close to me.

THERE YA GO.

BYE.

YOU GON' STARE AT THAR SUDS, AIN'T GON' WARSH THEYSEL.

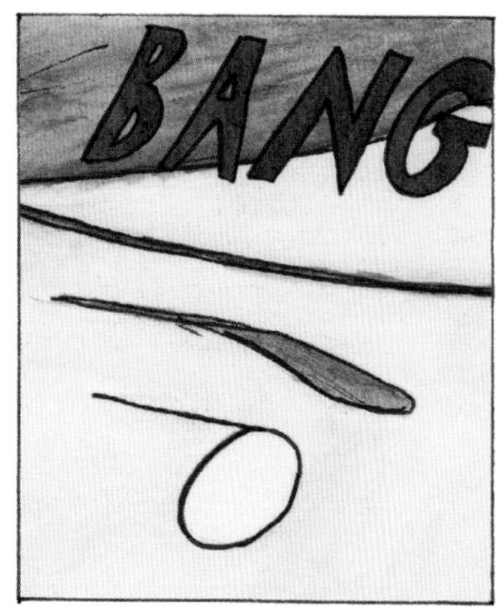

I Recommend...
by Nicky

Chapter 1

Being yourself is shit. No one likes you, and that's because of who you are. So be someone else! It's that easy, idiots!

YOU REALIZE YOU'RE ONLY EIGHT BULLS FROM YOUR D.E.? YOU COULD HAVE THIS IN THE BAG, LIKE, TOMORROW.

WE SHOULD SCHEDULE IT. LIKE A C-SECTION.
SUNSET, THE HOUR OF FIRE!
WE COULD SEND INVITATIONS.
OR DUSK! THE HOUR OF SHADOW.

NICKY, WILL YOU SCORE THIS FOR ME?

LIBBY, I DON'T NEED TO SCORE THIS. . . .

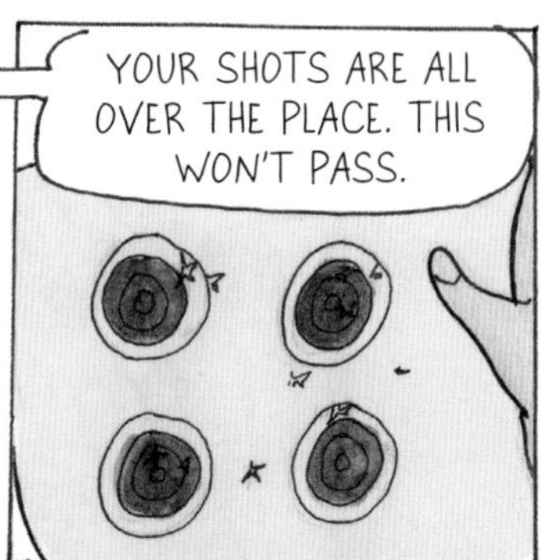
YOUR SHOTS ARE ALL OVER THE PLACE. THIS WON'T PASS.

WELL, I'M SORRY IT'S NOT ALL ONE-HOLE-GROUPS LIKE MAGGIE'S. BUT WILL YOU **FUCKING SCORE IT?**

WHOA.

I — I'M SORRY.
I DON'T KNOW WHY I SAID THAT.

HEY, MAGGIE, WHY DON'T YOU . . . GO TAKE A WALK OR SOMETHING?
SOB

ME?

I was supposed to have another two hours of peace from my insane feelings. But now, thanks to Libby, I was being flung out into them. It felt like a tether being snapped. It felt like, if I couldn't shoot, then I had to see Erin immediately or something worse would snap.

I kept thinking about this pair of girls from two summers ago, Beth and Ellie. They were obsessed with horses, in a way the rest of us had outgrown and found kind of boring. So we were already used to vaguely ignoring them.
Then these rumors started going around about them doing weird things, like wearing each other's underwear and sneaking out of their tents at night to go off together. Supposedly Hailey Ann saw them zipped together in the same sleeping bag once — completely naked. I don't know if any of it was true — it probably wasn't. But they were pretty much ostracized until the end of camp.
And neither of them ever came back.

This was Wolf Trackers, the nature skills class. It was really unpopular. Usually only one or two girls showed up.

WHATCHA DOIN?
RUB RUB
JUST . . . SCRATCHING MY BACK.
LIKE A BEAR.
BUT WHAT WERE YOU STARING AT?
NOTHING!

LET'S SEE. . . .
BETHANY, DON'T.

WHOA.

ARE YOU . . . ?
OH MY GOD.

WAIT.

I —

YOU —

NO —

ERIN?

HA HA HA HA
HA HA

HA HA HA HA

HA HA HA HA

FOR CHRIST SAKE
BETHANY SHUT UP

DRAG

It was obvious. That was the worst possible thing she could have said. If it was obvious to Bethany, who I was barely even friends with, then it could be obvious to anyone. So I was doomed.

IF YOU ASK MOI, NO
HOMOPHOBIA IS SO PASSÉ.
THIS CAMP IS LIKE A WORM HOLE
TO THE DARK AGES! AT MY SCHOO
JUST LIKE IN TITANIC. BUT THERE W
WASN'T EVEN FUNNY! BUT I LAUGHED
SHOULD GO TO PROM TOGETHER, LIKE T
AND HIS MOM TOLD HER MOM, AND TH
AN'T PRAY THAT SHIT AWAY!
EAN, TO EACH THEIR OWN, RI
ASICALLY GWEN STEFANI IS
I WAS LIKE, WHO ASKED YOU

PROBABLY A SAGITTARIUS
COULD DRAW WITH HIS FEET,
AND EVERYONE KNEW HE WAS GA
A REALLY UNFORTUNATE HAIRCUT
THE PROM THEME WAS "JUNGLE MADNES
DROWNED HIMSELF IN A JACUZZI SO
WEARS A RAINBOW ON THURSDAYS
OWN WAY, LIKE SEXUALLY, YOU KNO
AND THEIR PARENTS FREAKED OUT A
GAY IS PRACTICALLY BANNE
IN 10,000 YEARS, WHO KNO
PROBABLY BEST FRIENDS!

FREAKS, GOSH, HMM. WHAT MAKES YOU SAY THAT?
COULD IT BE THEIR LOVE OF EQUINES?

OR THE FACT EVERYONE KNEW THEY WERE —

LESBIANS.

WELL, YEAH, THAT . . .
BUT THEY WERE FREAKS TO BEGIN WITH, SO . . .
I MEAN, HORSES OR GIRLS, PICK ONE.

BUT YOU COULD TOTALLY PULL THIS OFF, IF YOU JUST . . . DON'T BE A FREAK!

I'M ALREADY A FREAK.

I'M FOLLOWING HER AROUND LIKE A STALKER.

IT'S ONLY STALKING IF YOUR VIBES ARE BAD. WHAT ARE YOUR VIBES?
HUH?

LIKE, ARE YOU SENDING HER BEAMS OF POSITIVE ENERGY?
. . . NO.

WELL YOU SHOULD! COME ON, LET'S MEDITATE TOGETHER. IT'LL HELP YOU NOT FREAK OUT AS MUCH.

IMAGINE THE SKY IS ON FIRE, THE FIRE OF TRANQUILLITY, AND YOUR MIND IS THE FIRE OF POSITIVITY. AND IT'S PURPLE AND IT'S IN THE SHAPE OF A DOG.
Bethany was clearly bonkers and didn't seem to care that she'd just yanked a huge secret out of me. And whether it stayed a secret wasn't even up to me anymore — it was up to her.

THERE, I FEEL BETTER. YOU?
SURE. NOW LISTEN, YOU CAN'T TELL ANYONE.
THIS IS A SECRET. IT'S NOT, LIKE, A FUN FACT.
FUN FACT: MAGGIE LOVES ER —
BETHANY

SLAM
. . . MAGGIE?

AREN'T YOU SUPPOSED TO BE IN RIFLE?

UM, YEAH. BUT I WAS EXILED.
EXILED?!

WE'LL TAKE YOU.
WOLF TRACKERS WELCOMES THE DISPOSSESSED.

COME ON, WE'RE LEARNING FIRE-BUILDING.

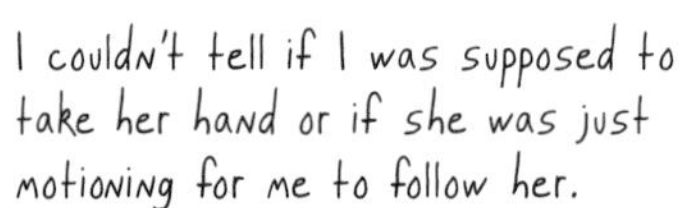
I couldn't tell if I was supposed to take her hand or if she was just motioning for me to follow her.

I kept staring at it, trying to decide.

GEEZ, COME ON.
YANK

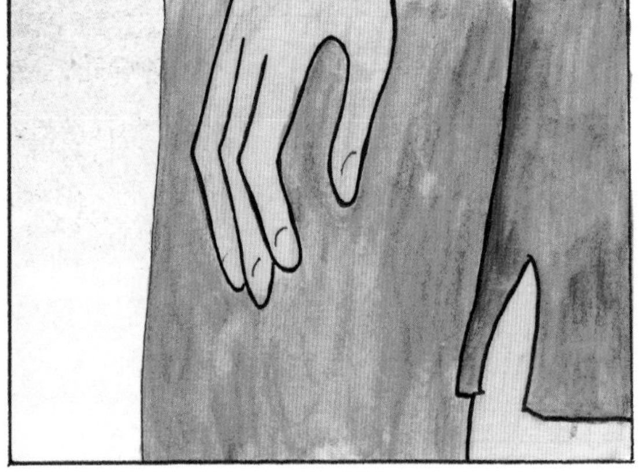

CHAPTER 5
What Are the Odds
SO . . .
IS THERE A TYPE OF WOOD THAT BURNS BEST?
SCOFF
ACTUALLY THAT'S A GOOD QUESTION.
SOME WOODS BURN HOTTER THAN OTHERS. SOME THROW SPARKS.

RED OAK IS BEST FOR THIS AREA.
HEY ERIN.
YOU KNOW MAGGIE HERE IS, LIKE, A GENIUS.
HM?
WELL I'M NOT SURPRISED.
SHE KNOWS SO MANY FUN FACTS.
TELL US A FUN FACT, MAGGIE.
UM . . .
MONKEYS CAN EAT WITH THEIR TAILS.
IF YOU EAT A MONKEY, IT COUNTS AS CANNIBALISM.
MONKEY BARBERS EXIST.
CATS HAVE . . . TAILS.
THE BEARD OF BLACKBEARD WAS ACTUALLY DARK BROWN.
CATS ARE BETTER THAN DOGS.
BLACKBEARD BROUGHT THE SIAMESE CAT BREED TO AMERICA.

DID YOU KNOW . . .

IN 1922, A GIRL DROWNED AT THIS VERY CAMP.

THAT . . .

AND SHE WAS SUCH A LONER, IT WAS SIX HOURS BEFORE ANYONE EVEN NOTICED SHE WAS GONE.
SO NOW HER SPIRIT HAUNTS TENT 22, AS PAYBACK FOR HOW EVERYONE IGNORED HER BACK IN THE DAY.

OK . . .
EXCEPT THAT'S NOT A FUN FACT. THAT'S A GHOST STORY.

BUT IT WAS GOOD! I WISH MORE PEOPLE TOLD GHOST STORIES IN THE MIDDLE OF THE DAY.

DING DING DING

Y'ALL GO CLEAN UP FOR DINNER.
I'LL PUT THIS OUT.

HEY MAG, IF YOU GET EXILED AGAIN, COME BACK TO WOLF TRACKERS.
ANYTIME.

THANK YOU! I WILL!
MAYBE I'LL EXILE MYSELF!

EXILE IN THE FOREST. VERY MYTHOLOGICAL.

YES! VERY!

SAY FAREWELL, MAGGIE.
BYE . . .

"ANYTIME." WOW. SHE LOOOOVES YOU.

NO.
NO NO NO. DO NOT EVEN TEASE ME LIKE THAT.

I'M SURE SHE'S NOT, YOU KNOW, GAY.

LIKE YOU'RE QUALIFIED TO SAY.
YOU DIDN'T EVEN KNOW YOU WERE GAY.

I NEVER SAID—

OK, OK, LET'S NOT HAVE A BIG CRISIS.

WHAT DO YOU EVEN CARE IF I HAVE A CRISIS OR NOT?

I THINK YOU'RE JUST WAITING FOR ME TO EMBARRASS MYSELF SO YOU CAN LAUGH YOUR HEAD OFF.

WELL SO WHAT?
AT LEAST SOMEONE WOULD BE LAUGHING.
. . . WHAT DOES THAT MEAN?

YOU KNOW. **SMILING?** HAR-DEE-HAR?
YOU ARE WAY TOO SERIOUS, MAGGIE THRASH.
YOU CAN'T EVEN PRETEND TO BE A BACKSTREET BOY WITHOUT IT BEING THE MOST SERIOUS THING IN HISTORY.
IT'S CAMP. IT'S SUPPOSED TO BE **FUN.**
WELL EXCUSE ME FOR NOT HAVING THE TIME OF MY LIFE.
EXCUSE ME FOR HAVING THE SLIGHTEST SENSE OF HUMOR.
COME ON, IT'S FUNNY. YOU LIKE **ERIN.**
PLUS YOU'RE A MIDGET.
YOUR FACE! YOUR MIDGET RAGE!
HA HA HA HA HA
HEY GUYS. WHAT'S SO HILARIOUS?

JUST . . . HOW SHORT MAGGIE IS.

YUP. LOTTA MILEAGE ON THAT ONE.

WELL, I'LL SCAMPER OFF NOW. SEE YA *ANYTIME.*

I LOOKED FOR YOU AT THE RANGE. NICKY SAID YOU RAN OFF?
I WAS AT WOLF TRACKERS.

SINCE WHEN ARE YOU INTO WOLF TRACKERS?
IT WAS JUST A SPONTANEOUS THING.

At dinner I saw Bethany talking to Erin. I knew she probably wasn't going to blab with a hundred girls around, but I was still so nervous I could barely eat.
Harry Potter

IT'S KIND OF CUTE. SHE'S LIKE A LIBBY WANNABE.
SHE'S LIKE, DEAR DIARY, WHY DOESN'T LIBBY LIKE ME? MAYBE IF I SHOOT RULL GOOD, SHE'LL BE MY FRIEND.

I'D HAVE MY D.E. BY NOW IF SHE'D QUIT SUFFOCATING ME. SHE'S DOING IT ON PURPOSE.

SHE'S SUCH A SHOW-OFF. NICKY SHOULD MAKE HER STOP SHOOTING.

TOTALLY. BAN HER FROM THE RANGE TILL SHE LEARNS SOME FUCKING SPORTSMANSHIP.

IF SHE GETS HER D.E. BEFORE ME, I'LL KILL MYSELF.
YOU SO SHOULD.
YOU **SO** SHOULD.

BETHANY.

WHAT WERE YOU SAYING TO ERIN?

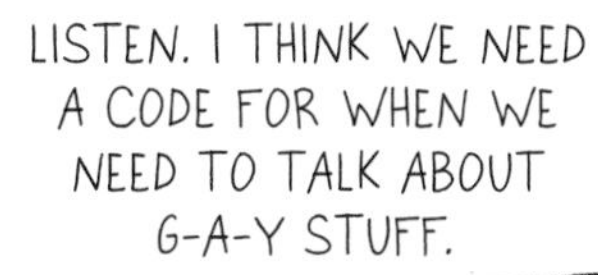
LISTEN. I THINK WE NEED A CODE FOR WHEN WE NEED TO TALK ABOUT G-A-Y STUFF.

LIKE, "THE BANANA FLIES AT MIDNIGHT."

OK . . .
THE BANANA FLIES AT MIDNIGHT.

COOL!
LET'S MEET SOMEWHERE TONIGHT, AFTER PRAYERS.
LIKE WHERE?

We quickly realized there was nowhere to go.

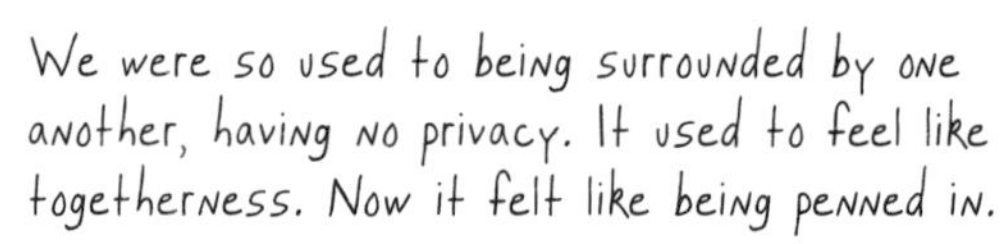
We were so used to being surrounded by one another, having no privacy. It used to feel like togetherness. Now it felt like being penned in.

PLURAL NOUN.
PENISES.

We ended up in the middle of the tennis court with a blanket thrown over our heads.

HIDING IN PLAIN SIGHT.
WE RULE!

SO. HANGIN' WITH MY TINY GAY FRIEND.
OH MY GOD.

I DON'T WANT TO BE A GAY FRIEND. I JUST . . . WISH I WERE A GUY.
A GUY?
YEAH, LIKE A SLOG BOY.

THEN I COULD GIVE HER A FLOWER, OR TAKE HER OUT . . . ON THE BARGE.
EW! ERIN WOULD NEVER GO OUT ON THE BARGE WITH A SLOG BOY.

OR ANY GUY! I'M TELLING YOU, SHE LIKES GIRLS.
BETHANY, I KNOW YOU THINK YOU'RE BEING NICE. BUT PLEASE DON'T —

I'M NOT BEING NICE! I CAN PROVE IT. I HAVE EVIDENCE!
YOU DO?

I GAVE HER A QUIZ.
A QUIZ?
WANNA TRY IT?
. . . SURE.

CIRCLE OR SQUARE?
HUH?
JUST SAY ONE.
UM, SQUARE?

BLACK OR WHITE?
. . . BLACK.
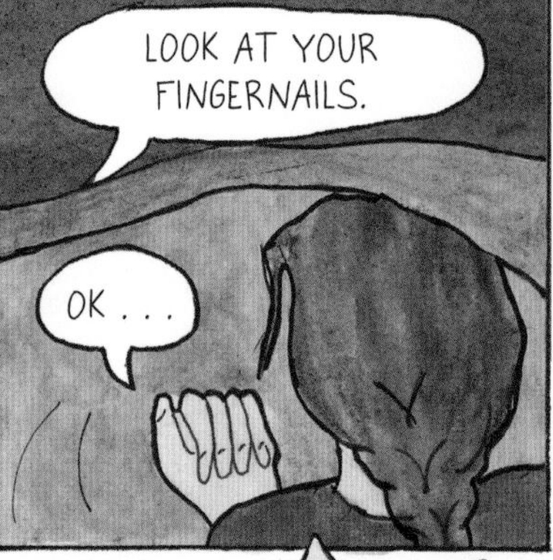
LOOK AT YOUR FINGERNAILS.
OK . . .

NOW LOOK AT THE SKY.

THE RESULTS ARE IN!

YOU LIKE GIRLS.
. . . REALLY.

I'M SERIOUS! IT'S A REAL QUIZ!

IF YOU LIKE BOYS, YOU'RE SUPPOSED TO ANSWER "CIRCLE" AND "WHITE."

AND YOU LOOK AT YOUR NAILS LIKE THIS.

AND YOU LOOK AT THE SKY LIKE THIS. WITHOUT RAISING YOUR CHIN.

BOTH YOU AND ERIN GOT A ZERO OUT OF FOUR.
DING
LIKE, IDENTICAL.

UGH, TAPS.
DING
SEE YOU TOMORROW!
DING

Obviously I didn't think Bethany's quiz results were definitive. But she'd said Erin and I answered every question the same. What were the odds of that?

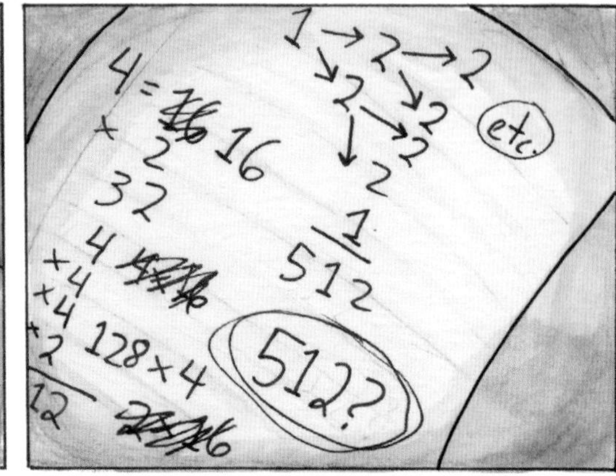

I decided to ask my brother, who was a math genius. He was in the hospital that summer, getting surgery on his ribs and sternum. He had a sunken chest, which is a genetic deformity where your ribs grow abnormally, caving in around the heart.

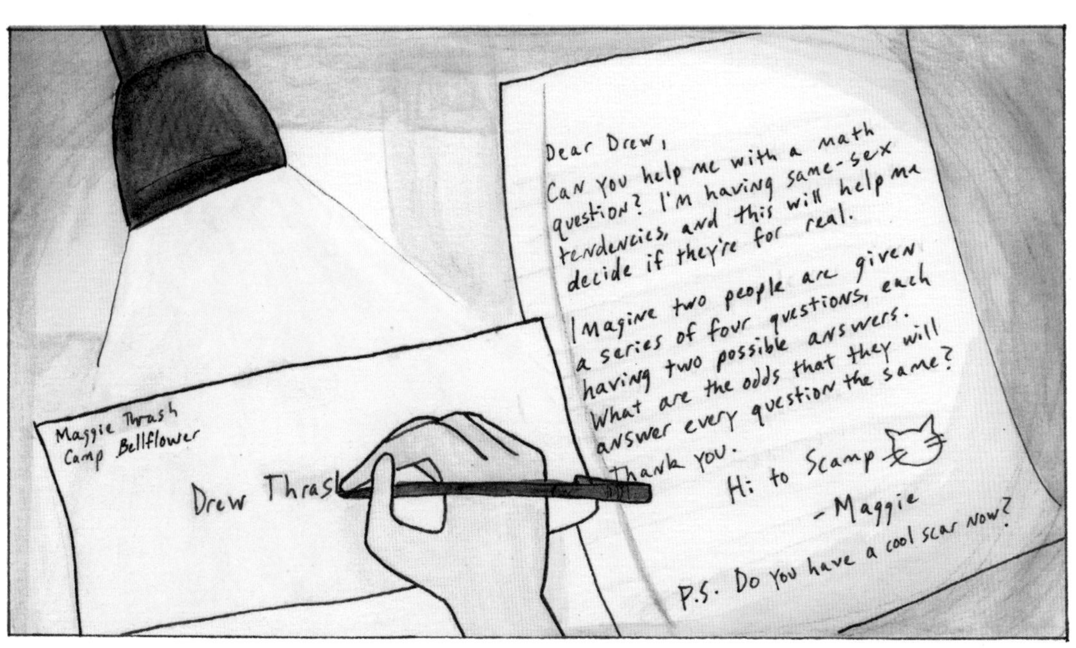
Dear Drew,
Can you help me with a math question? I'm having same-sex tendencies, and this will help me decide if they're for real.
Imagine two people are given a series of four questions, each having two possible answers. What are the odds that they will answer every question the same?
Thank you.
Hi to Scamp
- Maggie
P.S. Do you have a cool scar now?
Maggie Thrash
Camp Bellflower
Drew Thrash

WHERE ARE YOU GOING? PUT YOUR LEASH ON, YOU BAD GIRL.
I'M JUST GOING TO THE MAILBOX.

MAIL

Now I had to wait at least two weeks for an answer.

CHAPTER 6
Predators
HOW DO YOU DO THIS?

YOU SURE YOU DON'T WANT TO COME TO THE BLUE RIDGE?
MY PARENTS WOULD INVITE YOU.
NO THANKS. I LIKE STAYING HERE.

IT'S PEACEFUL WITH EVERYONE GONE.

On Sundays all the parents came to visit. Everyone wore Lilly Pulitzer dresses and went to the Blue Ridge Inn in town to have lunch and get manicures. My parents never came because Atlanta was too far away.

BYE, LITTLE ORPHAN! I'LL BRING YOU A CHOCOLATE BAR.

The last barge pulled away, and it was so quiet I could hear a guitar playing across junior camp.
I knew it was her.

I really wanted to stalk her, but with camp so empty, I knew she'd spot me in a second.

It made me realize how much I relied on being one amid a hundred girls — of the flock, concealed by the flock. Now the flock was gone, and without it, I was a single white shirt, standing out against the green tents and green grass.

HI.

HEY! YOU DIDN'T LEAVE?
NO, I NEVER LEAVE.
LIKE THE GHOST OF TENT 22?
YEAH! I SHOULD GO HAUNT THE BARGE.
NO WAY! HAUNT ME!
I MEAN, HANG OUT WITH ME.
OK!
GOD, IT'S SO HOT TODAY.
I KNOW, I'M GLAD WE CAN JUST . . . SIT AROUND.
IS THERE A WAY I COULD TOUCH HER WITHOUT HER NOTICING?
CHRIST, DON'T THINK LIKE THAT. HOW PERVERTED CAN YOU BE?!
DON'T TOUCH HER. DON'T TOUCH HER. DON'T TOUCH HER.

CONTROL
GRAB
LOOK.

OUR HANDS ARE THE SAME SIZE.

THAT'S ODD. I'M SO MUCH TALLER THAN YOU.

I HAVE VERY OGRE-ISH HANDS FOR MY BODY TYPE.

I . . .
I HAVE TO FILL OUT THESE DUMB CAMPER REPORTS BY 10:30.
I WISH I WERE AMBIDEXTROUS.

LET ME FILL THEM OUT! I'M RIGHT-HANDED.

UM . . . OK! IF YOU WANT TO.

JUST CIRCLE "SATISFACTORY" FOR EVERY QUESTION.
OK!
WAIT, WHAT'S THE LAST ONE?
"DEMONSTRATES BELLFLOWER SPIRIT"?
UM . . .

HALT
. . . ERIN.

I THINK MAGGIE NEEDS TO GO BACK TO SENIOR CAMP.

UM . . . OK. I'LL WALK HER.

I'LL WALK HER.

GO AHEAD.
YOU KNOW, MAGGIE, I'M GLAD WE HAVE THIS CHANCE TO CHAT.
YEAH, UM, I REALIZE THAT LOOKED STRANGE BACK THERE, BUT I SWEAR —
NO, NO NO. IT'S NOT THAT.
DON'T EVEN WORRY ABOUT THAT. IT'S NOT YOUR FAULT.
. . . HUH?
IT'S THIS THING WITH YOU AND RIFLE.
ME AND . . . RIFLE.

PEOPLE ARE STARTING TO THINK YOU'RE A BIT OF A SHOW-OFF.
JUST SO YOU KNOW.
PEOPLE LIKE WHO?

LIKE LIBBY?
IT DOESN'T MATTER **WHO.**

IT'S ONE THING TO EXCEL. IT'S ANOTHER TO SHOW OFF AND MAKE PEOPLE FEEL BAD ABOUT THEMSELVES.
I'M NOT — I DON'T —

I GET THAT THIS D.E. STUFF IS A BIG DEAL. BUT IS IT WORTH CLIMBING A MOUNTAIN IF YOU HAVE TO STEP ON SOMEONE TO DO IT?

WELL, IF THAT PERSON WOULD GET OUT OF MY WAY, I WOULDN'T HAVE TO STEP ON THEM.
SWEETIE, THERE'S NO "MY WAY" AT CAMP.

IT'S OUR WAY, GIRL! WE'RE A SISTERHOOD!
SOUNDS LIKE LIBBY'S WAY TO ME.
SLAP!

MAGGIE, CHILL. THERE'S NO ROOM FOR HOTSHOTS HERE. I THINK YOU SHOULD BACK OFF THE RANGE, AND LET LIBBY CATCH UP ON HER TARGETS.
BACK OFF? IN THE JUNGLE, YOU DON'T ASK A TIGER TO BACK OFF. YOU EITHER RUN FAST ENOUGH OR YOU GET EATEN.

SO THIS IS THE JUNGLE, THEN? AND YOU'RE A TIGER? AND THE REST OF US ARE JUST TOTALLY INSIGNIFICANT?
WELL . . . NO . . .
LISTEN, I DON'T KNOW HOW NICKY'S BEEN RUNNING THE RANGE, BUT DOWN HERE WE DON'T LET OUR EGOS RUN AMOK.
AND WE DON'T ACT BETTER THAN EVERYONE ELSE JUST BECAUSE WE SHOT A FEW ONE-HOLE-GROUPS.
SORRY.
THERE'S A PEACH! NOW, DON'T WE FEEL BETTER?
YES, TAMMY.
AND DON'T WORRY ABOUT THE OTHER THING.
WHAT OTHER —?
WITH ERIN. WE'LL GET IT SORTED OUT.
GET IT SOR — WAIT, WHAT?

The counselors' lodge was the most guarded, off-limits place in camp. No campers were ever allowed inside. We weren't even supposed to set foot on the porch.

KNOCK
KNOCK

. . . YEAH?

UM, IS NICKY THERE?

NO, IT'S HER DAY OFF.
WHAT ARE YOU DOING HERE?

SORRY, I JUST —
I THINK YOU SHOULD GO BACK TO YOUR TENT.

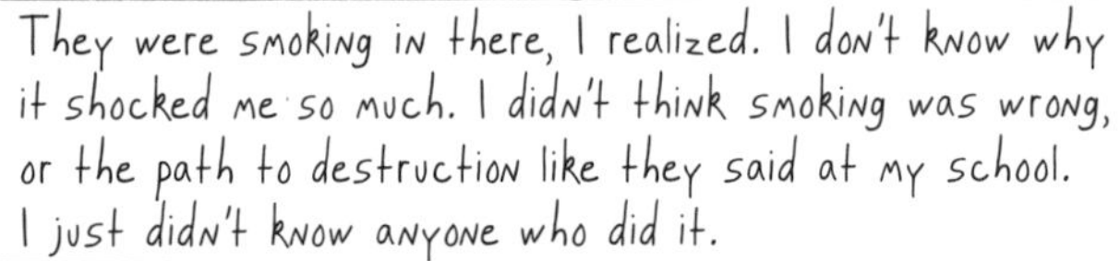
They were smoking in there, I realized. I don't know why it shocked me so much. I didn't think smoking was wrong, or the path to destruction like they said at my school. I just didn't know anyone who did it.

SLAM

SO DID YOU ENJOY YOUR DAY OF SOLITUDE?
YEAH . . .

PART OF IT, ANYWAY.

PSST! MAG!
I SNEAKED YOU TWO, SO YOU CAN GIVE ONE TO ERIN.
BETHANY, I CAN'T GIVE CANDY TO A COUNSELOR.
I'D PRETTY MUCH BE ASKING TO GET IN TROUBLE.
SHE WOULDN'T GET YOU IN TROUBLE.
OBVIOUSLY.
WHY NOT?
DO YOU HAVE A SUGAR DISPENSATION?
UH . . .
WHATEVER, HAVE YOUR LITTLE SECRET SOCIETY.
IT'S NOT A SOCIETY. IT'S . . .
A BACKSTREET BOYS FAN CLUB.
SNORT
WHACK
AND ERIN'S IN IT?
. . . YEP.
THAT'S SURPRISING. I WOULDN'T HAVE TAKEN HER FOR THE BOY BAND TYPE.
WELL THAT'S EXACTLY THE MAGIC OF BACKSTREET BOYS.
THEY TRANSCEND ALL THAT STUFF.

SSSNAP

MAGGIE?

WHAT ARE YOU DOING HERE?

I CAN'T SLEEP. IT'S TOO HOT.

I'M JUST GOING TO PRETEND I CAN'T SEE YOU.

BECAUSE IF I SEE YOU, YOU'D BE IN HUGE TROUBLE.

EVERYTHING IS DARK.

MAAAAAGGIEEEE

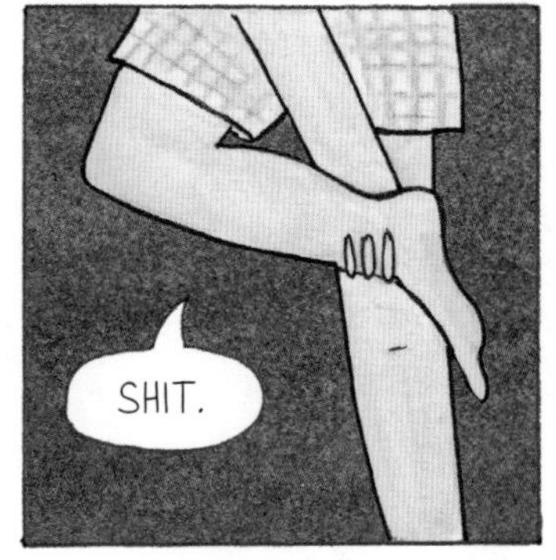
SHIT.

THERE YOU ARE!

ARE YOU AWAKE?

I'M AWAKE, I'M AWAKE.

SHE COULD HAVE DROWNED.

I SAVED HER LIFE.

WE HEAR THE WHIP-O-WILL SINGING ABOVE

MAGGIE
SLAM

MAGGIE, MAGGIE'S IN LOVE!

OH MY GOD.

IS BETHANY OUTING ME?

AT BREAKFAST?

TO THE WHIP-O-WILL SONG?

. . . JUST LIKE A DOVE! MAGGIE, MAGGIE,

MAGGIE LOVES . . .

LUKE!

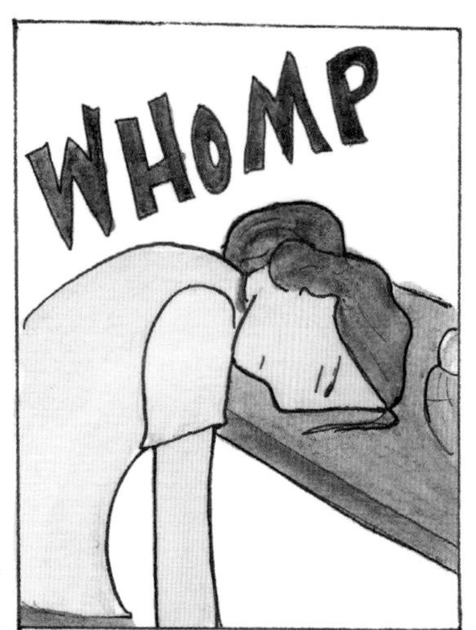
WHOMP

MMM?

BETHANY!

MAAAAGGIE!

WHY ARE THOSE LITTLE FIENDS CHASING YOU?
I HAVE NO IDEA.
GO ON — SAVE YOURSELF.

MAAAGG
. . . YES?

THIS IS FROM ERIN.
SHE SAID NOT TO LOOK IN YOUR EYES.
Maggie
SHE SAID YOU'D PUT A CURSE ON US.

Maggie

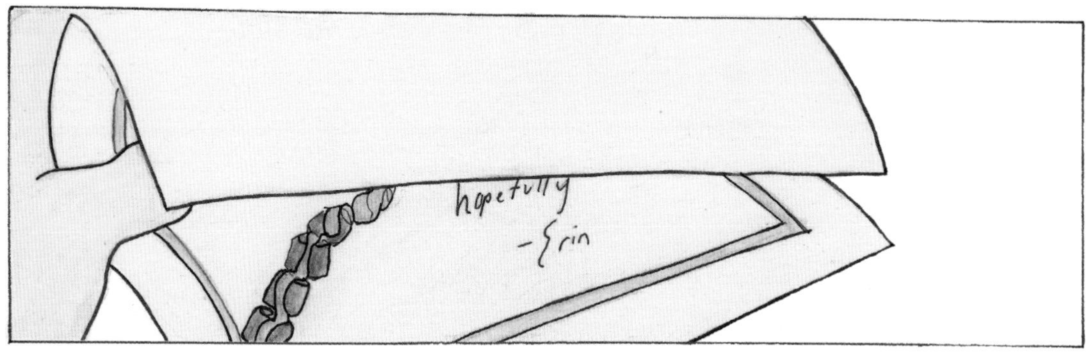
hopefully
-Erin

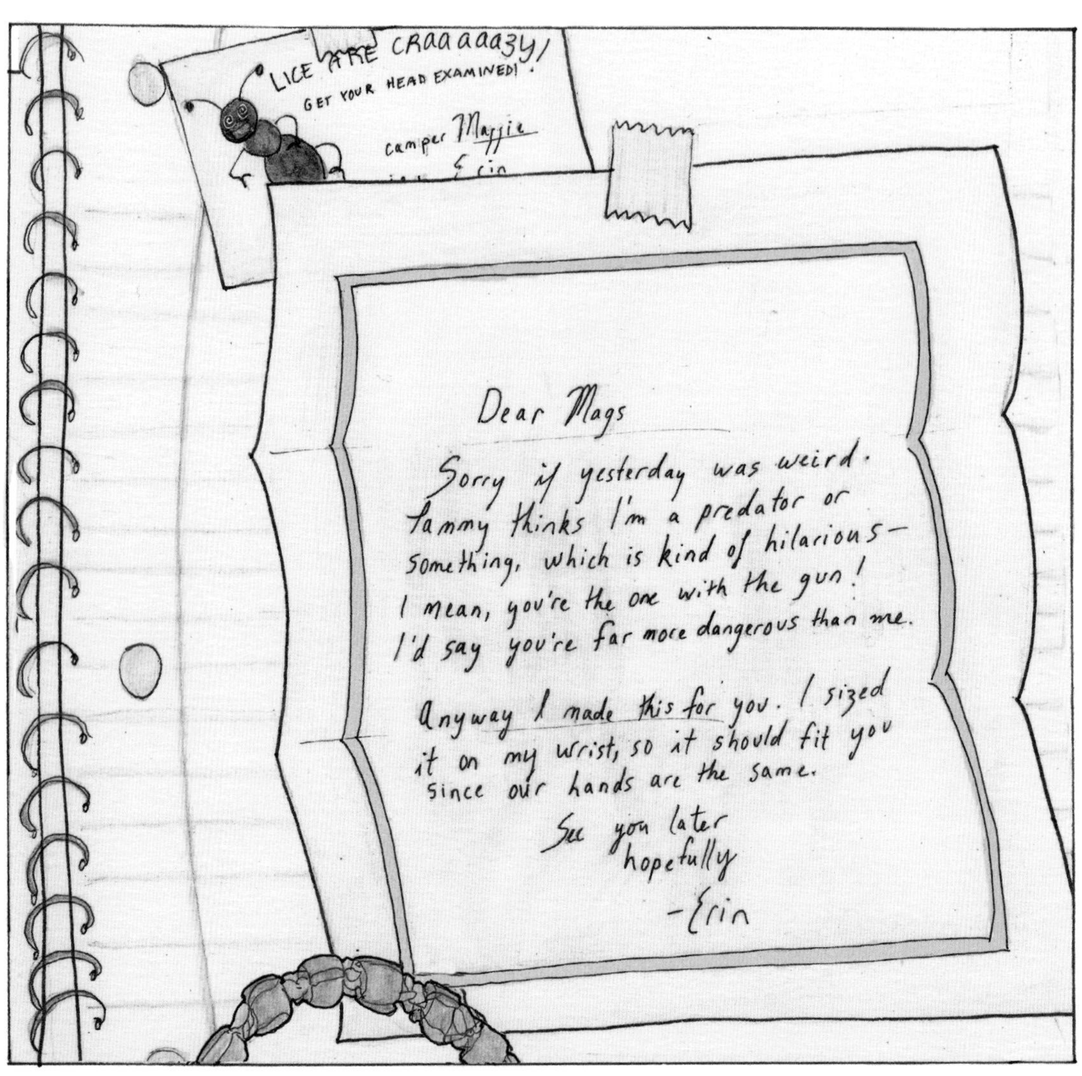

Dear Mags

Sorry if yesterday was weird. Tammy thinks I'm a predator or something, which is kind of hilarious— I mean, you're the one with the gun! I'd say you're far more dangerous than me.

Anyway I made this for you. I sized it on my wrist, so it should fit you since our hands are the same.

See you later
hopefully

-Erin

CHAPTER 7
Tough Girls

DID YOU HEAR ABOUT HER AND TENNIS BETHANY?

APPARENTLY THEY WERE ON THE TENNIS COURT, BASICALLY NAKED **UNDER A SHEET.**

JESUS, REALLY?

BLYTHE SAID THEY WERE PRETTY MUCH DOING IT WITH **A RACKET.**

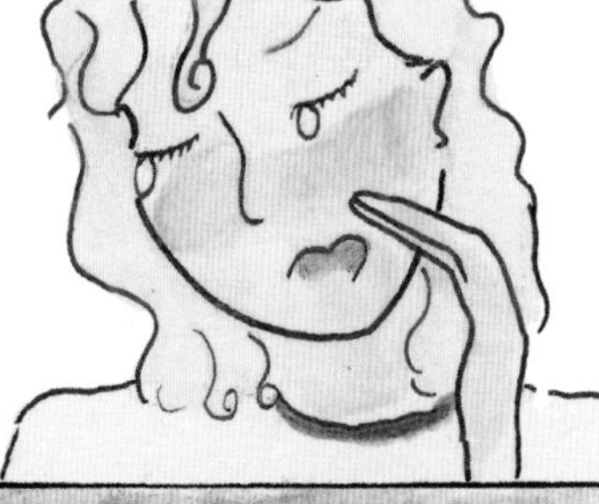

THAT IS SO NASTY.

IT'S JUST WHAT HAPPENS WHEN YOU TAKE BOYS AWAY. EVERYONE GOES CRAZY.

APPARENTLY MAGGIE'S OBSESSED WITH VAGINAS AND BETHANY'S OBSESSED WITH TENNIS, SO THEY HAVE, LIKE, AN ARRANGEMENT.

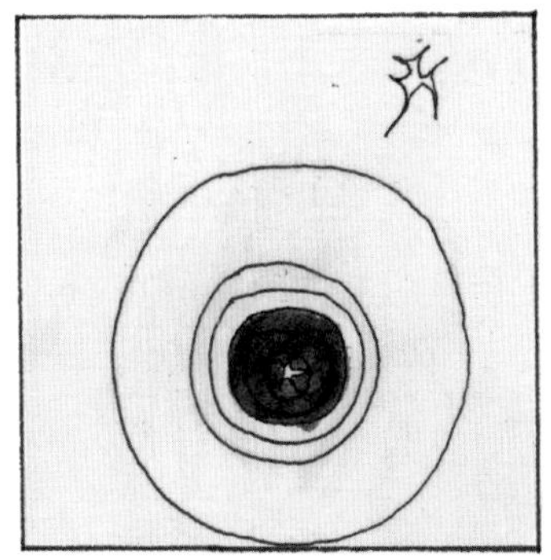

?!

DID YOU SHOOT MY TARGET?

OOPS.

STAY OFF MY SIDE.

SNICKER
WATCH THIS.
YOU DON'T EVEN NEED A GUN TO MESS WITH HER HEAD.

HURL

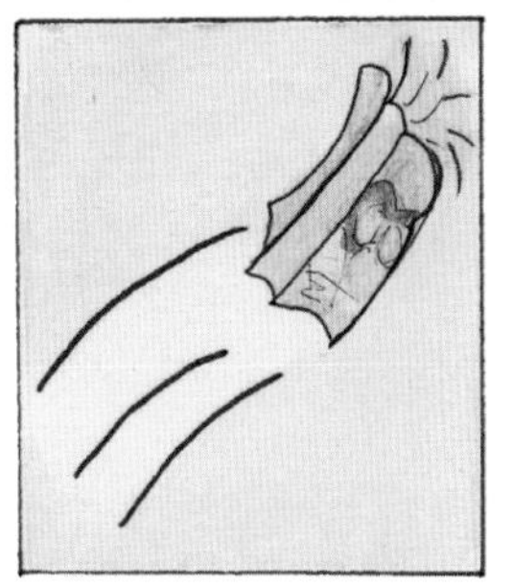

SMACK
follow your heart?

OH SHIT!

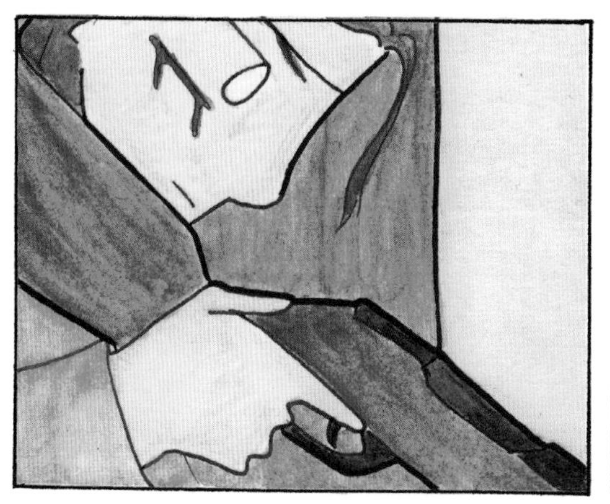

CAN I SERIOUSLY NOT LEAVE YOU ALONE FOR FIVE MINUTES?

AND WHAT THE HELL HAPPENED TO MAGGIE'S FACE?

WE'RE JUST SHOOTING.

Once every summer, we were invaded by boys. It was a tradition with the camp across the river. The boys were usually nice but not that impressive. I always hoped that a moody Kevin Richardson type would manifest amid the sea of khakis and bowl cuts and lacrosse tans, but he never did. And this year, if he did, I doubted I would even care.

YOUR LIPS ARE REALLY CHAPPED, SO YOU NEED A GLOSSY FINISH.

I was used to the way everyone threw themselves on top of each other all the time. Girls held hands and shaved each other's legs and called each other sweetheart. But maybe I wasn't supposed to do that anymore because now everything I did would turn into some gross rumor.

WHY ARE YOU SUCH A SOURPUSS? AREN'T YOU EXCITED FOR BOYS?
NO. I WISH THEY WOULD LEAVE US ALONE.

WHEN THEY SHOW UP, I'M GOING TO SCARE THEM AWAY.

OMIGOD. WE SHOULD DRESS LIKE SLUTS AND SCARE THE SHIT OUT OF THEM!

I MEANT LIKE JUMP OUT AT THEM FROM BEHIND A TREE.

YOU CAN'T WEAR THAT, ABIGAIL.
TA-DA!

WELL, I'M NOT WEARING A LILLY.
I'M TIRED OF LOOKING LIKE A PRISSY BOUQUET.

MAGGIE, YOU SHOULD DRESS TOUGH WITH ME.
WHAT DOES "TOUGH" MEAN?

IT MEANS, HEY BOYS, MAYBE I'LL KISS YOU, OR MAYBE I'LL BEAT THE SHIT OUT OF YOU.
C'MERE AND FIND OUT.

JUST TRUST ME AND PUT THESE ON.

PANTS? YOU'RE WEARING PANTS?
CALM DOWN, MARY KELLY. IT'S NOT THE COLLAPSE OF SOCIETY.
I'M GONNA GET SOME HAIR SPRAY. THE TRICK WITH HAIR IS **CONTROLLED DISHEVELMENT.**
HEY.
HEY!

WOW. YOU LOOK CUTE.
THANK YOU!

BUT WHAT HAPPENED TO YOUR FACE?
OH GOD. LIBBY THREW A BOOK AT ME.

SHE'S GOING INSANE BECAUSE I'M BETTER THAN HER.

YEAH, I HEARD YOU'VE BEEN DOMINATING THIS YEAR. . . .
SCOOT OVER.

SO, SHOOTIN' GUNS . . .

IS THAT SOMETHING YOU'RE SERIOUS ABOUT?

I DON'T KNOW IF I'M SERIOUS. . . . NICKY SAYS I COULD GO TO OLYMPIC TRIALS OR SOMETHING. . . .

BUT BETHANY ALWAYS SAYS I'M TOO SERIOUS. SO . . . I GUESS I CAN'T DECIDE WHICH TO BE.

WELL, MAYBE IT'S NOT SOMETHING YOU DECIDE. MAYBE IT'S SOMETHING YOU FEEL.

IF IT FEELS SERIOUS, IT IS SERIOUS.

I BETTER GO.
MY CAMPERS ARE FREAKING OUT.

YOU KNOW, **BOYS.**

BOYS.

FEAR

SEE THAT GUY? HE WANTS YOU.
WHAT? I DON'T EVEN KNOW HIM.
HE'S LACEY'S COUSIN, AND HE'S A RIFLE GOD. HE HAS A DOUBLE D.E.
BANG
SO LACEY TOLD HIM YOU WERE A RIFLE GODDESS! AND YOU'LL HAVE LITTLE RIFLE BABIES TOGETHER.
WELCOME TO OUR CAMP, GENTLEMEN. REMEMBER . . .
I'M ALWAYS WATCHING!

WE SHOULD SLAM PUNCH TILL WE GET A PSYCHOTIC SUGAR RUSH.
THAT IS SUCH A GOOD IDEA.

SLAM

GULP

CRUSH

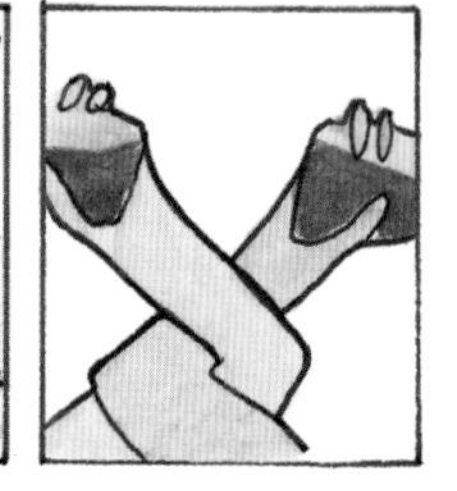

HEY.

I HEARD YOU'RE THE TOP SHOOTER AROUND HERE.
UH-HUH.

HOW MANY TARGETS DO YOU HAVE TILL YOU GET D.E.?
TWO.

TWO? YOU GOTTA NAIL THAT BITCH! SEAL THE DEAL!

WELL SHE WAS JUST ABOUT TO BEFORE YOU DICKHEADS INVADED US!
BETHANY!

YOU KNOW I HAVE A DOUBLE D.E. — RIFLE AND SHOTGUN.
I HEARD.
I COULD SHOOT THOSE PESKY TARGETS FOR YOU.
. . . EXCUSE ME?

I'D BE HAPPY TO. JUST TAKE ME TO THE RANGE. IT'LL BE OUR LITTLE SECRET.
WOW, I DON'T NEED SOME DUDE TO CHEAT FOR ME. I'M DOING JUST FINE.
SURE YOU ARE.

WOULD YOU LIKE A DEMONSTRATION?
I WOULD!

YANK

DRAG

HEY NICKY, WILL YOU TAKE US TO THE RANGE?
HUH?

WE WANNA SHOOT.
NOW?!
YEAH, IT'S STILL DAYLIGHT. JUST A FEW TARGETS.
ABSOLUTELY NOT.

WHAT IS WRONG WITH YOU? JUST GO DANCE AND BE NORMAL.
SHOVE

SO DO YOU USE AN ARM SLING WHEN YOU SHOOT?
SOMETIMES . . . I SHOOT PRETTY FAST, SO I DON'T USUALLY NEED ONE.

I BET YOU SHOOT REAL FAST.
ROLL

ARE YOU A RIGHT-EYE OR A LEFT-EYE?
RIGHT. I WEAR AN EYEPATCH ON THE LEFT.

SEXY!

YOU THINK SHE'S CUTE?

WHO?
THAT CAMPER. THAT LITTLE FOURTEEN-YEAR-OLD CAMPER.
SHE'S FIFTEEN.
ANYWAY, I'M TAKING A BREAK.
YOU DO THAT.
I HAVE TO GO.
HAVE YOU MET LIBBY? SHE'S FANTASTIC.

MAGGIE.

WE SHOULD GET OFF THIS PORCH BEFORE SOMEONE SEES US.

NOT THAT WE CAN'T BE SEEN TOGETHER. . . .

IT'S JUST THAT WE'RE BOTH SO POPULAR . . .

PEOPLE WILL TRY TO TALK TO US

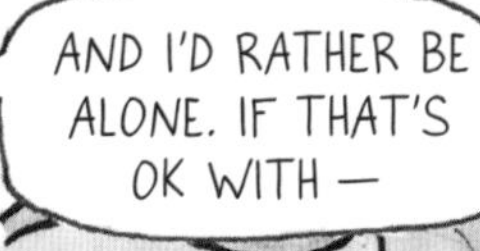
AND I'D RATHER BE ALONE. IF THAT'S OK WITH —

YEAH, LET'S GO.

There's a reason two people sneak out of a dance together. It's to make out. Abigail did it every summer. But I wasn't Abigail, and Erin wasn't some guy, so it was impossible to say whether the standard practices applied. Maybe we were just getting fresh air. Maybe that was an actual thing and not just what people said to disguise what they really wanted.

I THINK YOU WOULD LIKE BOULDER. . . .
HAVE YOU EVER LEFT THE SOUTH?
NO . . .

HUH, WHAT IF I KIDNAPPED YOU? WHAT IF I JUST SHOWED UP AT YOUR HOUSE AND DROVE YOU AWAY?

IT WOULD LITERALLY BE A KIDNAPPING. AN ADULT TRANSPORTING A MINOR ACROSS STATE LINES.

IT'S NOT LIKE I'D BE STUFFED IN A TRUNK AND TIED UP WITH A BALL GAG IN MY MOUTH.

JESUS, MAGGIE!

SNAP

IS THAT ABIGAIL?

OH GOD, I BETTER GO BREAK IT UP.

WAIT.

. . . YEAH?

MAYBE . . . WE COULD JUST SCARE THEM AWAY. WITH ANIMAL SOUNDS.
LIKE WOLVES HOWLING?
I CAN DO A PRETTY GOOD BIRDCALL. . . .
OH YEAH? LET'S HEAR IT.
whoooooo
WHOA.
HOW DO YOU DO THAT?
JUST HOLD YOUR HANDS LIKE THIS AND BLOW DOWN.
LIKE THIS?
SPPP TTS
HERE, TRY ON MY HANDS.
JUST . . . BLOW DOWN.
phht-
whoo

whooooo

HEY.
THEY'RE PLAYING YOUR SONG.
HM?
LISTEN.
You are my fire...

I BET EVERYONE IS THINKING ABOUT YOU RIGHT NOW.
WHICH MEANS YOU BETTER GO.
BEFORE THEY NOTICE YOU'RE GONE.
AND THAT I'M GONE.

the one desire...
believe when I say
HEY.
SHE STOLE YOUR DUDE.
I'M DEVASTATED.
HEY, DID YOU HEAR THERE'S A RUMOR ABOUT US?
WHAT?! I DIDN'T TELL ANYONE ABOUT E-R-I-N, I SWEAR.
NOT ME AND . . . E-R-I-N. ME AND **YOU.**
PEOPLE SAW US ON THE TENNIS COURT UNDER THE BLANKET.
NOW THEY'RE SAYING WE'RE PERVERTS.
YOU KNOW WHAT'S ACTUALLY PERVERTED?
THIS SONG. I MEAN, WHAT "WAY"? DOWN ON ALL FOURS?

BUT I WAS THINKING. MAYBE THIS RUMOR IS A GOOD THING. BECAUSE THE MORE LIES PEOPLE TELL, THE EASIER IT IS TO HIDE WHAT'S REALLY TRUE.
LIKE, SAY THERE ARE A HUNDRED RUMORS ABOUT YOU, AND YOU JUST REFUSE TO CONFIRM OR DENY ANY OF THEM. MAYBE THERE'S ONE TRUE THING HIDDEN IN THERE . . .
BUT NO ONE WOULD EVER KNOW.
EXCEPT THEN HOW DO YOU BE A TRUE PERSON? LIKE, IN YOUR LIFE?
YOU DON'T.
YOU JUST . . . INHABIT THE WEB OF LIES FOREVER.
THAT SOUNDS DUMB AND EXHAUSTING. WOULDN'T IT BE EASIER TO JUST SHOW PEOPLE WHO YOU ARE?
NO.

YOU'RE INVITED
CHAPTER 8
Over the River and
Through the Woods
at the hour of shadow (7pm)
come watch Maggie shoot
her Distinguished Expert
NRA
FOREVER
WE HEAR THE -O-WILL SINGING ABOVE. CAITLIN
FOR YOU.

GEE, I'M FLATTERED YOU REMEMBER THAT I EXIST.
HM?

I NEVER SEE YOU ANYMORE. YOU'RE ALWAYS SHOOTING OR HANGING OUT WITH THAT WEIRD TENNIS GIRL.

WHATEVER, FORGET IT.
. . . SORRY.

I'M JUST FEELING A TAD SUICIDAL TODAY.
IF I HEAR THE WHIP-O-WILL SONG ONE MORE TIME I MAY SERIOUSLY END IT ALL.

EVERYONE'S IN LOVE!
EVERYONE'S DEMENTED.

IT'S LIKE, LANDON SETS MY HEART **FREE,** BUT DANNY SETS MY HEART **ON FIRE.**
WHICH IS TRUE LOVE?

I always appreciated Shannon's cynical ways, but now they made me nervous. Would she see any difference between my obsession with Erin and Abigail's obsession with Danny the garbage guy? Probably not.

Solvent
HEY,
LIBBY WANTS TO TALK TO YOU.
OKAAAY.
AND SHE'S REALLY SENSITIVE, UNLIKE YOU.
SO TRY TO BE NICE FOR FIVE SECONDS.
HI.
WHAT IS THIS?
UM . . . IT'S JUST A JOKE. YOU WEREN'T SUPPOSED TO SEE IT.
I DON'T UNDERSTAND YOU. HOW CAN YOU BE SO NICE ONE MINUTE AND SO MEAN THE NEXT?
NICE? WHEN WAS I ESPECIALLY NICE?

YOU GAVE ME CAM!

. . . WHAT'S CAM?

CAM. LACEY'S COUSIN. WHO'S AMAZING, BY THE WAY.
OH.

BUT THEN YOU PULL THIS AND MAKE ME FEEL ALL SHITTY AGAIN.

SORRY. BUT IT'S NOT MY JOB TO MAKE YOU FEEL GOOD ABOUT YOURSELF.

YES, IT IS! THAT'S THE EXACT DEFINITION OF FRIENDSHIP!

WE'RE.
NOT.
FRIENDS.

ONLY BECAUSE YOU'RE SUCH A BITCH.

YOU WERE A BITCH WAY BEFORE ME. I WAS JUST RESPONDING.

WELL WE'RE BOTH BITCHES NOW! HAPPY?

GUN SHACK

THIS IS THE ONLY THING IN MY LIFE
AND YOU'RE TAKING IT.

YOU HAVE GREAT HAIR.

SHUT UP.
YOU DON'T GET IT. YOU'RE JUST A KID.

COME ON, YOU'RE LIKE ONE YEAR OLDER THAN ME.

WELL OBVIOUSLY ONE YEAR CAN MAKE A HUGE DIFFERENCE.
BECAUSE IF YOU WERE MORE MATURE, YOU'D GET IT.

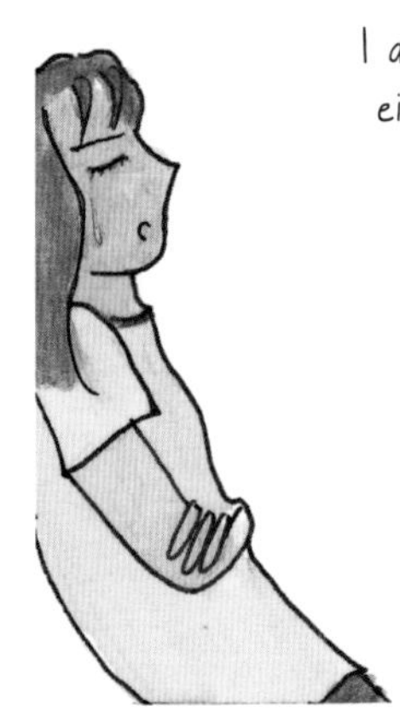

I didn't know what it felt like to be mature. I didn't think Libby knew either — the way she cried and whined all the time seemed pretty childish to me. But she was right that I could have been more magnanimous about it. Even now, I didn't really care about her feelings. I mostly cared that she was making me look bad. Maybe if I did something gracious and mature, Erin would hear about it and be impressed. Which I think I realized was possibly the most immature reason to do something nice.

HOW MANY TARGETS DO YOU HAVE LEFT?
EIGHT.
WELL, I HAVE ONE. BUT I'LL HOLD OFF ON SHOOTING IT IF YOU CAN CATCH UP.
THEN WE'LL SHOOT IT TOGETHER. AT THE SAME TIME.
YOU WOULD DO THAT FOR ME?
. . . SURE.
THANK YOU!
EVERYONE IN JUNIOR CAMP SAYS YOU'RE EVIL. BUT THEY'RE WRONG.

Toward the end of every summer, the senior campers crossed the river to see a play at the community theater in town. The plays tended to be about old-timey values — a fishing hole was often a prominent set piece. But the night wasn't really about the play. It was about the excitement of leaving camp and being in the outside world again. Then, inevitably, you remembered that the outside world is full of old people and hammy theater and that you really weren't missing much.

HI.
HI.

SORRY TO BE ALL COVERT. . . .
I JUST WANTED TO SEE YOU BEFORE YOU LEFT.
COME HERE.

WOW. YOU REALLY ARE SHORT.

HANG ON.
LIFT

THERE.

HOW DOES IT FEEL
TO BE TALL?

FEELS GOOD! VERY POWERFUL.
IF I WERE THIS TALL, I'D PROBABLY BE A MEGALOMANIAC.
ACTUALLY I THINK MEGALOMANIACS ARE HISTORICALLY SHORT.

I don't know
how I knew this,
but I understood
somehow that it was
my responsibility to
make this kiss happen,
if it was going to happen at
all. She'd gone as far as she
could; that was clear to me.

IS THAT THUNDER?

It was such a delicate moment,
that's all it took to break it.

But I didn't feel confident that I was reading the moment correctly. I mean, I knew, I really knew. But it was too easy to tell myself I was delusional.

Her fingers brushed my neck for a second.

Then she dropped her hand and it was over.

MAGGIE!
YOU'RE LATE.
SORRY.
DID YOU KIIIISS?
BETHANY, SHUT UP!
YOU TOTALLY DID. I CAN TELL.
WHAT DO GIRLS TASTE LIKE?
UM, RAIN? THEY TASTE LIKE RAIN.
MAGGIE, YOU MORON.
IT'S RAINING.
The thrill of leaving was even more short-lived than usual. The world was cold and gray and wet, and there was nothing out there that I cared about.

I knew I shouldn't have let Bethany believe that this kiss happened. But in a way, the fact that her lips hadn't touched my lips seemed inconsequential — a dumb technicality. But of course I knew it wasn't dumb. Because until it happened, we both had plausible deniability.

OVER THE RIVER
AND THROUGH THE WOODS
BOX OFFICE
The play was about a long-suffering guy who lived with all four of his Italian grandparents. They interfered constantly in his dating life, force-feeding him pasta and wise proverbs.
EGLI E MAL SOADO CHE NON VUOL ODIRE.
NONE SO DEAF AS THOSE WHO CANNOT LISTEN.
WHAT? SAY THAT AGAIN?

I wasn't really paying attention. I was thinking about her and swearing to myself that the next time we were alone, I was going to act. It would finally be definitive, one way or the other.

HEY MAG, LOOK.
HM?

HAVE YOU EVER SEEN A HUGER WEDGIE?

LIKE I SAID, GRANDPA . . .

I ALREADY ATE!

SNORT

HA HA HA

COLLECT YOURSELVES OR EXCUSE YOURSELVES. NOW.

OH MY GOD . . .

HEY, DO YOU HAVE ANY MONEY? WE COULD BUY A SNICKERS.

I BET HE'D GIVE YOU ONE FOR FREE.
WHAT? NO WAY.
WAY! WHEN GIRLS WEAR RED, BOYS' BRAINS EXPLODE.
CONCESSIONS

OK. LET'S GO GET IT, THEN.
WHAT? I WAS KIDDING.

MAY I HELP YOU?

GOT ANY SWEETS FOR A SWEETIE?
. . . WUT?

I'M SORRY, I JUST — I JUST REALLY NEED A SNICKERS.
SMACK

HA HA HA HA

. . . HERE.

HOLY SHIT

THANK YOU, CONCESSIONS BOY!
CONCESSIONS

I CAN'T BELIEVE THAT WORKED.
HE'S PROBABLY OBSESSED WITH YOU NOW.
HE'LL PROBABLY BE YOUR STALKER.

I DON'T CARE.
I'M NOT SCARED OF BOYS.

SHOULD WE GO BACK IN?
NO. LET'S SEE HOW FAR WE CAN PUSH CONCESSIONS BOY.

YOU SHOULDN'T USE YOUR GIRLISH POWERS FOR EVIL, MAGGIE.
THAT'S NOT WHAT I'M DOING.

YES, IT IS.

THEN THE GRANDPA DIED.
WHICH GRANDPA?
THE LITTLE ONE, WHO SAID LIFE WAS BEST SERVED AL DENTE.
IT WAS SO SAD.
I NEED EVERYONE TO STAY ON THE BUS.
WHAT'S HAPPENING?
GOD. IT LOOKS LIKE THE RIVER ROSE FIVE FEET.
Actually it rose eight feet. Eight feet in four hours.

CHAPTER 9
Stranded
I'd never seen the river like this. It was rushing so fast, like it was trying to pour itself out.
WE CAN'T TAKE THE BARGE OUT. THE CABLES WILL SNAP.
THIS IS A NIGHTMARE.
JUST . . . SPLIT THE GIRLS UP. WE'LL COME BACK IN THE MORNING.
WHERE ARE WE SUPPOSED TO PUT THEM?
CALL PARENTS IN THE AREA. CALL ANYONE WITH A MOUNTAIN HOUSE.

CAN MAGGIE COME IN MY GROUP?

YOUR TENT'S GOING TO DANNY'S CABIN. IT'S FOURTEENS ONLY.
MAGGIE HAS TO STAY WITH THE FIFTEENS AND SIXTEENS.

THAT'S STUPID. WHY?

UMM . . .

She wouldn't say it, but clearly they wanted to keep the older campers away from the Slog Boys. I found it kind of disturbing, the insinuation that Danny or Luke could see us as WOMEN, as actual objects of desire. That we needed to be separated from them for our own good. I guess it was flattering. . . . But mostly it felt embarrassing and weird.

IT'S ALL RIGHT — MAGGIE CAN GO.
SHE'S FINE.

OMIGOD. IS THAT LIKE A LESBIAN PERK? THAT THEY TRUST YOU AROUND DUDES?
I GUESS. . . .

I. HATE. YOU.

Danny's family's cabin was ten miles upriver. It was me, Bethany's tent, plus some counselors I didn't know very well. Everything smelled like mildew and balsam pine needles.

DANNY, DO YOU HAVE SOMETHING THE GIRLS CAN SLEEP IN?
SURE.

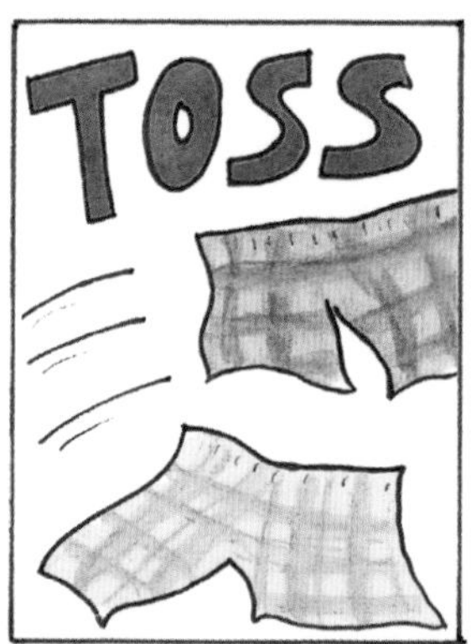
TOSS

WE'RE GONNA SLEEP IN HIS UNDERWEAR?
JUST BE COOL AND PUT IT ON.

Y'ALL.

54oz
Skittle

WHERE ARE THE COUNSELORS?

SEE HOW THEY ALL HAVE MUGS?
YEAH.

IT MEANS THEY'RE **DRINKING.**
WHAT?!?

THEY DON'T WANT US TO SEE WHAT'S INSIDE.
MAYBE IT'S COFFEE.

THEN WHY IS THERE NO STEAM?
I FISH THEREFORE I AM

ARE WE GOING HOME?
I MEAN, BACK TO CAMP?
THE RIVER'S STILL TOO HIGH. WE'RE CHECKING EVERY FOUR HOURS.
People
SO . . . WHAT ARE WE SUPPOSED TO DO?
I DUNNO. DO WHAT YOU WANT.

DO YOU KNOW HOW TO COOK BREAKFAST?
LIKE, POP-TARTS? YOU JUST PUT THEM IN THE TOASTER.
WHAT ABOUT . . . EGGS BENEDICT?
HA. GOOD LUCK WITH THAT.
Y'ALL,
DANNY HAS *THE SECRET GARDEN.*
The Secret Garden
IT'S MY **SISTER'S.**
I LOVE THAT MOVIE.
PUT IT IN.
IT'S BEEN FOUR HOURS.
ARE WE GOING?
THE GARDEN HAS SECRETS.
NOPE.

4 hours later

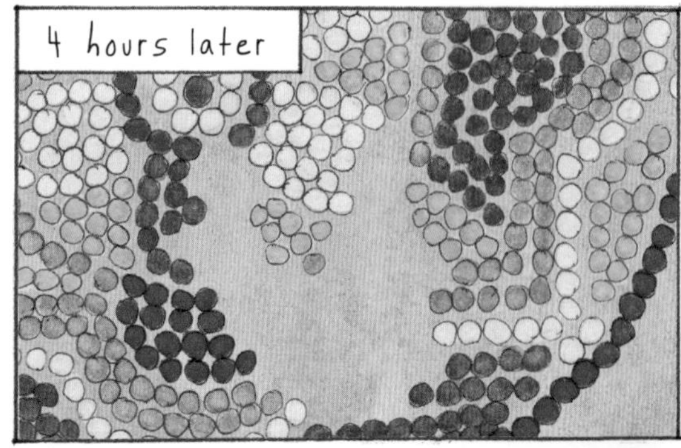
4 hours later

4 hours later
LET'S WATCH *THE SECRET GARDEN* AGAIN.

4 hours later
IT'S CALLED WUTHERIN, THE MOOR.
I HATE IT.

4 hours later
I THINK DANNY'S **DRUNK.**

4 hours later
BLOODY MARY
BLOODY MARY
BLOODY MARY
BLOODY MARY

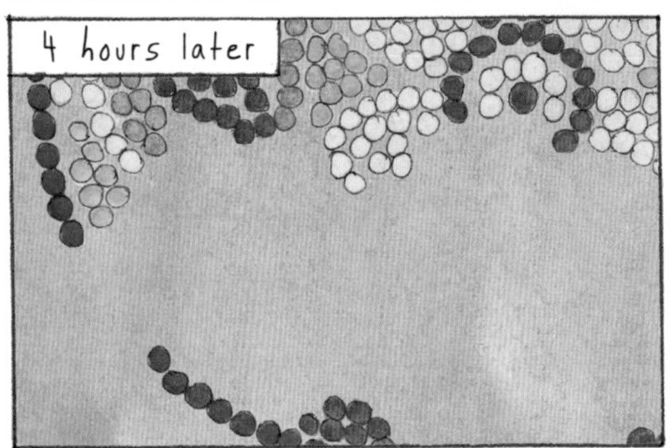
4 hours later

4 hours later

4 hours later
EGGS BENEDICT!

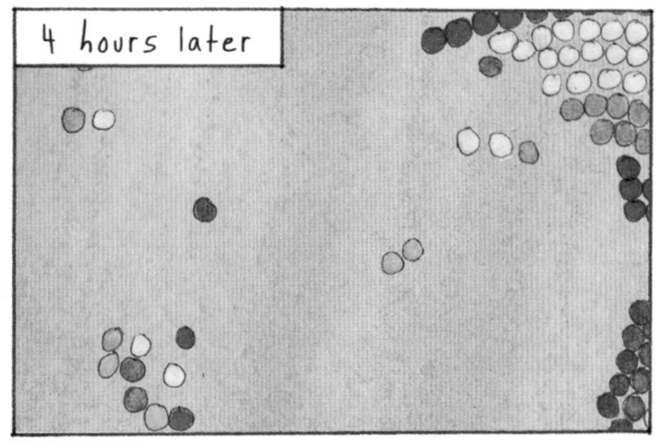
4 hours later

4 hours later
AND THE TAMPON WAS IN THERE FOR A **WEEK.**

4 hours later
SEC-RET
SEC-RET
SEC-RET
SEC-RET
SEC-RET
GAR-DEN
GAR-DEN
GAR-DEN
DEN
DEN

4 hours later
THE GARDEN **IS** MAGICAL!

4 hours later

4 hours later
RESPECT THE RAIN.
IT'S THE OCEAN REINCARNATED.

4 hours later
EAT IT.

POKE
POKE
STOP IT.
POKE
TAMMY'S GOING TO THE STORE FOR US. Y'ALL NEED ANYTHING?
CAN SHE GET SOME CETAPHIL AND A TOOTHBRUSH?
WHEN I WAS A KID, I HATED BRUSHING MY TEETH.
NOW I DON'T HATE ANYTHING.
I DON'T **FEEL** ANYTHING.
OKAAAY . . .
WHAT'S WITH ANSLEY?
SHE JUST NEEDS HER ZOLOFT.

ZOLOFT?
IT'S FOR DEPRESSION.

ANSLEY HAS DEPRESSION?
YEAH.

A LOT OF PEOPLE DO.

Suddenly I really didn't want to be there anymore. It was ridiculous being stuck in this place, away from my gun, and away from Erin. There weren't even that many days of camp left. And here they were, just disappearing. The entire summer was disappearing. And at the end of it, Erin would go back to Colorado and forget about me, all because I never made myself clear.
WHERE ARE YOU GOING?
DANNY'S ROOM.
WHY?
TO BE ALONE FOR FIVE MINUTES.
WHY?
SLAM

the slammer
KIDZ Write! stationery
I love you
I love you
I love you

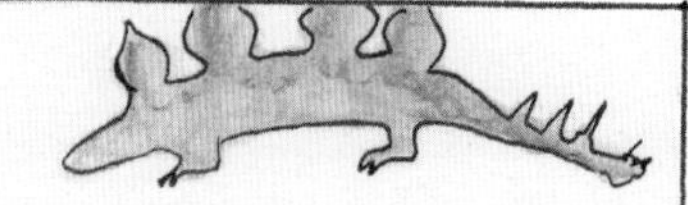

Dear Erin,
Have you ever met someone where when you're near them it feels like you're going to die

OH MY GOD.

half hour later

KNOCK, KNOCK.

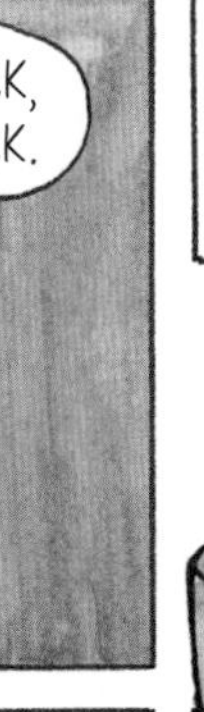

I GOT YOUR STUFF.
WHAT ARE YOU DOING IN HERE?

JUST DOODLING. YOU KNOW . . . DOODLES.

BUT NOW I'M DONE.

YOUR FACE WASH LOOKS LIKE JIZ.

THAT IS SO IRONIC.

JIZ FACE, JIZ FACE.

MAGGIE, CAN I TALK TO YOU?

. . . SURE.

SHRUG

CAN Y'ALL CLEAR OUT, PLEASE?

SIT DOWN.
OK . . .

IS SOMETHING WRONG?

YOU SHOULDN'T STEAL OTHER PEOPLE'S STATIONERY.

YOU SHOULDN'T GO THROUGH OTHER PEOPLE'S TRASH.
CRUMPLE

MAGGIE, WHEN'S YOUR BIRTHDAY?
JUNE . . . JUNE 2ND.

SO?
YOU'RE BARELY FIFTEEN. YOU'RE BASICALLY STILL FOURTEEN.

SO IT'S GROSS. AND ILLEGAL. YOUR PARENTS COULD SUE US. DO YOU KNOW WHAT STATUTORY RAPE IS?
OH MY GOD.

THE LAW IS WORSE FOR QUEERS. DID YOU KNOW THAT, TOO?
DO YOU WANT ERIN TO GO TO JAIL?
I'M SERIOUS.

MY DAD'S A FEDERAL JUDGE. HE'D NEVER LET ERIN GO TO JAIL.

YOUR DAD'S A JUDGE?
SHIT!

Apparently that was the wrong thing to say.

I'M NOT TRYING TO SCARE YOU, SWEETHEART.
BUT IT'S MY JOB TO MAKE SURE EVERYONE FEELS SAFE.

I DO FEEL SAFE.
SHE'S NOT, LIKE, PRESSURING ME.

UNFORTUNATELY, YOU'RE NOT MY ONLY CONCERN.
EVERYONE **ELSE** NEEDS TO FEEL SAFE, TOO.
FROM YOU.

PARENTS DON'T SEND THEIR GIRLS HERE TO FROLIC AROUND IN YOUR LESBIAN FANTASY.

I MEAN, WE ALL KNOW ERIN'S . . . THAT WAY.
BUT SHE'S ALWAYS MANAGED TO CONTROL HERSELF.

WE'RE BOTH VERY CONTROLLED.
BELIEVE ME.

YOU BETTER BE. HAVE YOU HEARD OF "DON'T ASK, DON'T TELL"?
. . . YES.

WELL, IT'S THE LAW. AND IT MEANS NO ONE WANTS TO KNOW YOUR BUSINESS.
SO DON'T SHOVE IT IN PEOPLE'S FACES.
IT WASN'T IN YOUR FACE. IT WAS IN THE TRASH.

MAGGIE, DO YOU KNOW WHAT IT IS THAT MAKES CAMP SO SPECIAL?
. . . WHAT?
IT'S A PLACE WHERE GIRLS CAN BE TOTALLY INNOCENT AND FREE, MAYBE FOR THE LAST TIME IN THEIR LIVES.
DON'T RUIN IT FOR EVERYONE.
And that's when it finally stopped raining.

What was I doing before? Was I just . . . floating along? Maybe I was better off that way. Because what's ironic is that being in love doesn't actually make you happy. It makes it impossible to be happy. You're carrying this desire now. Maybe if you knew where it came from, you could put it back. But you don't.

CHAPTER 10
The Return of the Native

WELCOME BACK
SENIOR CAMP
DID YOU SEE HIM GET NAKED?
NO. IT WASN'T AN ORGY, ABIGAIL.
I BET IT TOTALLY WAS. YOU SO LUCKED OUT.
I WAS AT MARY ASHTON'S HOUSE.
HER MOM MADE US FOLD CHURCH LEAFLETS.
WE ATE **CREAMED CORN.**

If you ever got injured at camp, you were pretty much screwed. The nurse was an ancient old lady who believed the solution for everything was a vinegar soak. One summer a girl fell off her horse, and it was 20 hours before anyone called the hospital, even though she was screaming in pain and it turned out she'd broken her collarbone.

BOO-BOO SHACK

JUS' KEEP YA WEIGHT OWF IT, SUGAH. IT'LL RIGHT ITSELF IN NO TIME.

THAT LOOKS HORRIBLE.
WILL YOU HELP ME GET TO ARCHERY?

OW.
OW.

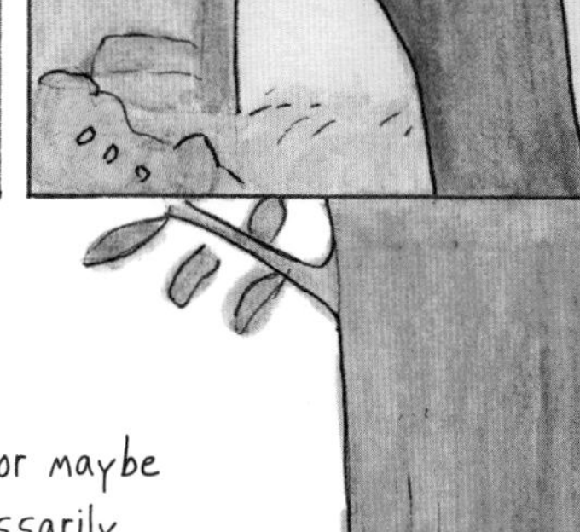

Maybe she hadn't seen me, or maybe she was busy. I didn't necessarily need to panic just because she didn't say hi, or even wave.

O town
WILL YOU PLEASE SHOOT A TARGET?
I PROMISED LIBBY I'D WAIT FOR HER.
THAT IS SO DUMB.
SHE'S MANIPULATING YOU!
MAYBE SO . . .

BUT I TOLD HER I'D WAIT, SO . . . I HAVE TO HONOR THAT NOW.
YOU WANNA HONOR SOMETHING?
HONOR YOURSELF. DON'T LET LOSERS WALK ALL OVER YOU.

PEOPLE WHO ARE BETTER DESERVE TO WIN, MAGGIE.

IT'S CALLED A MERITOCRACY. IT'S THE FAIREST SYSTEM ON EARTH.

STOP PEER-PRESSURING ME, NICKY.
I'M NOT YOUR PEER.

I'M OLDER AND WISER, AND I'M TELLING YOU TO SHOOT A DAMN TARGET.

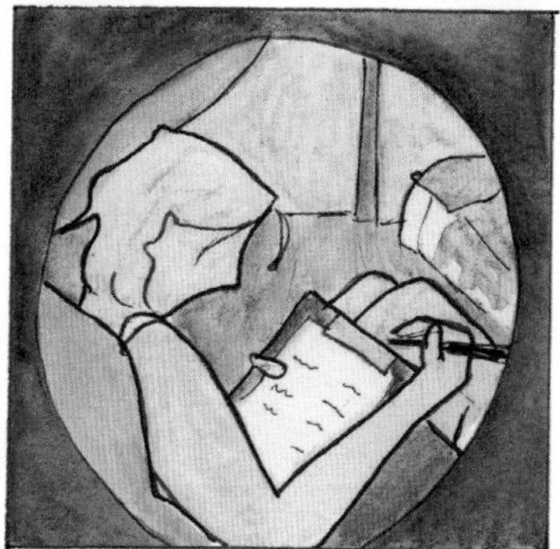

I'LL BE RIGHT BACK.

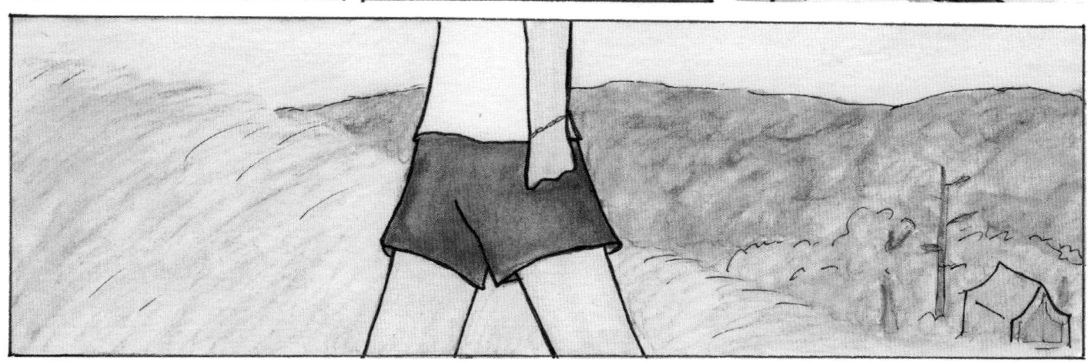

HI.

UM, CAN I HANG OUT WITH YOU?
I'M KIND OF BUSY.
COUNSELOR STUFF.
I COULD HELP YOU. . . .
NOT THIS TIME.
I'd planned to regale her with comical tales from my 82 hours at Danny's family's cabin, presuming she would at least acknowledge that I'd been gone. But she didn't.

UM, DID TAMMY SAY SOMETHING TO YOU?
BECAUSE SHE —

MAGGIE, IT'S NOT A GREAT TIME.
SORRY.

AND . . . I MEAN THAT IN A LARGER SENSE.

LIKE, HOW YOU KNOW IF SOMETHING'S IN THE STARS.
OR NOT.

WELL . . . YOU'RE THE ASTRONOMY MAJOR.

YEAH.
I AM.

ANYWAY . . . SEE YA.
SEE YA . . .

RAKE
RUMMAGE
Cream Cleanser
SPF 45

SLAM
I don't know why it occurred to me to do this. Maybe I saw it in a movie. I think the girl in *Legends of the Fall* does it right before she kills herself.
But I wasn't thinking of that at the time. I wasn't thinking of anything. It's just this mythological desire you have to suddenly — to be unrecognizable to yourself.
OH MY GOD.

BETHANY,
I NEED YOUR HELP.
HA HA HA
HA HA HA
HA HA HA
WAIT,
COME BACK!

SHANNON.
WHAT THE — ?

HELP.

YOU LOOK LIKE SHAWN FROM *BOY MEETS WORLD*.

WHOA.
CALM DOWN.
CRUMPLE

YOU DON'T LOOK LIKE *BOY MEETS WORLD*.
YOU LOOK LIKE . . . MRS. BRADY.

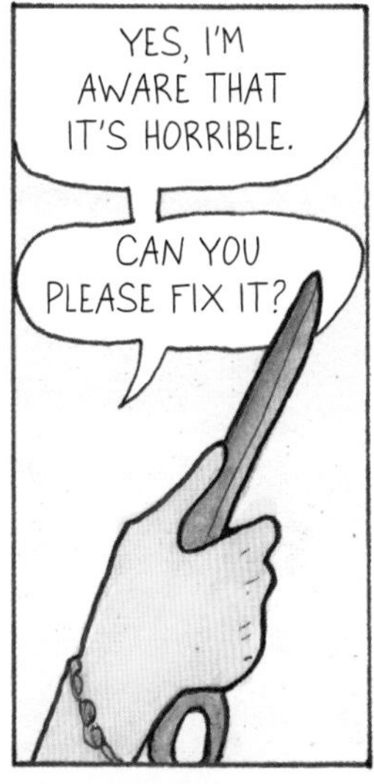
YES, I'M AWARE THAT IT'S HORRIBLE.
CAN YOU PLEASE FIX IT?

OKAAAY . . . LET'S DISPENSE WITH THIS LITTLE MULLET FOR STARTERS.

SNIP
SNIP

WHY IS IT SO POOFY ON TOP?

ALL RIGHT.
NOW SHAKE YOUR HEAD OUT.

NOT BAD!

BE CAREFUL, OR ELSE IT WILL FLOP INTO A BOWL CUT.

MUSS IT UP EVERY NOW AND THEN.
LIKE THIS?
YEAH.

SO . . . I BASICALLY JUST SAVED YOUR LIFE.
MY FEE IS THAT YOU HAVE TO TELL ME WHY YOU'VE BEEN SUCH A WEIRDO LATELY.

I REALLY DON'T WANT TO.
YOU **HAVE** TO.

OR WE'RE NOT FRIENDS ANYMORE.
I'M SERIOUS.

ARE YOU GAY?
THAT'S WHAT EVERYONE'S SAYING.

EVERYONE? WHO'S EVERYONE?

OH, JUST THOSE BITCHY SIXTEENS. NO ONE'S PAYING ATTENTION.

EXCEPT NOW THEY MIGHT. THIS HAIRCUT IS **QUITE** GAY.

OH, MY GOD. WHY DID I DO THIS?

NOT TO JUDGE YOUR PREDILECTIONS, BUT **BETHANY**?
SHE'S SO ANNOYING.

IT'S NOT BETHANY.
. . . IS IT ME?

ROLL
JUST CHECKING.

UGH.

UGH. POOR YOU.
YOU KNOW . . . YOU COULD HAVE TOLD ME.

I'M NOT LIKE EVERYONE ELSE HERE.
I THOUGHT YOU KNEW THAT.

I DO. I JUST . . .
I WAS AFRAID YOU WOULD THINK IT WAS LAME.

WHAT? BEING INTO CHICKS?

NO, JUST . . . BEING INTO ANYONE.

STOP STARING AT ME.
I'M MAKING SURE IT DOESN'T FLOP INTO A BOWL CUT.
I FEEL RESPONSIBLE!
MAGGIE! OMIGOD, YOUR HAIR.
IS IT, LIKE, TO TELL THE WORLD YOU'RE A L-E-Z?
NO NEED TO BE SO EXCEEDINGLY CRYPTIC, BETHANY. SHANNON KNOWS.
OH.
. . . THE TWO OF YOU SHOULDN'T STAND TOGETHER.
IT MAKES ME FEEL LIKE A SHRIMP.
Y'ALL COULD BEAT ME UP, LIKE, EFFORTLESSLY.

YEAH, BUT . . .
YOU COULD SHOOT US.
TRUE!
MAGGIE WON'T TELL ME WHO SHE'S IN LOVE WITH.
LIKE SHE'S INCAPABLE OF UTTERING HER NAME.

CAN I TELL HER?
JUST . . . WHISPER IT IN HER EAR. QUIETLY.

DON'T BOTHER FREAKING OUT.
IT'S PROBABLY ALREADY OVER.

LICE
GET YOUR HEAD EXAMINED!
camper Maggie
inspector Erin

MAGGIE.

SHHH.

FOLLOW ME.

I JUST WANTED TO SEE YOU. . . .

I LOVE YOUR HAIR.
THANK YOU.

. . . YOU SMELL NICE.

SO DO YOU.

WE PROBABLY SMELL THE SAME . . .

. . . JUST, LIKE, THE SMELL OF CAMP.

GOD, I'M SORRY I WAS SUCH A JERK EARLIER.
IT'S OK.

I JUST DIDN'T WANT YOU TO SEE.

. . . SEE WHAT?

MY ARMS ARE TURNING BLUE.

OH MY GOD.

IT'S SO EMBARRASSING.

I LIKE IT.
I THINK IT'S PRETTY.

YOU'RE SWEET.
PEOPLE MUST TELL YOU THAT A LOT.

NO.
NO ONE TELLS ME THAT.

I had no idea where I was, or where camp was. Usually when this happened, Mary Kelly or someone was right behind me. Usually I tripped over things and woke everyone up.

But this time . . . there was no one. It was creepy. It was like I was becoming this secretive and stealthy person, even in my sleep. And now I had to wait for the sun to come up to find my way back.

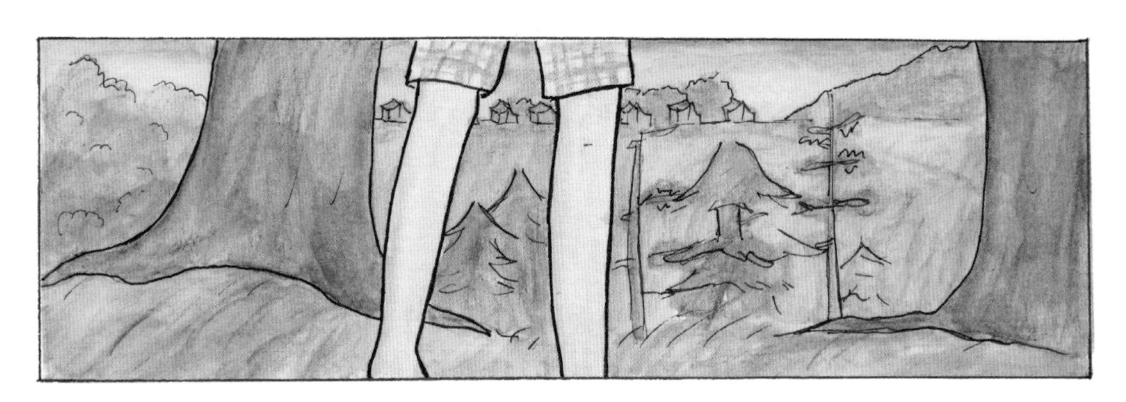

CHAPTER 11
One More Day

BOYS, AIR-CONDITIONING, EVERYTHING NOT SMELLING LIKE MILDEW. NO FREAKING CRICKET SOUNDS, MY DOGS, CHEERLEADING, *BUFFY*, MY CAR, NACHOS, WEARING WHAT I WANT, LIPSTICK, SLEEPING IN, MY BOYFRIEND LIKE, EVERY EPISODE OF *DAWSON'S CREEK*, DIET COKE, PEDICURES, MANI
You knew camp was almost over when everyone started talking about all the stuff they couldn't wait to do when they got home. And the daily schedule of things started to fall apart. Counselors stopped caring whether you showered at the appointed hour or skipped prayers or wore open-toed shoes. All those rigid rules seemed suddenly dumb, and you'd hear everyone saying, "What are they gonna do, send us home?"

MAGGIE.

I NEED TO TALK TO YOU. NOW.

OKAAAAY . . . HANG ON, LEXI.

WHAT HAVE YOU DONE TO YOURSELF?

SHRUG

ARE YOU HAVING A NERVOUS BREAKDOWN?

SHRUG

ONE MORE DAY, MAGGIE. THEN YOU CAN GO HOME AND SHAVE YOUR HEAD AND BE WHATEVER KIND OF FREAK YOU WANT.

TILL THEN I NEED YOU TO KEEP IT TOGETHER, OK?
. . . OK.

AND IF YOU'RE GOOD, I HAVE SOMETHING REALLY SPECIAL PLANNED.
WINK

IF I'M **GOOD**?
WHAT DOES THAT MEAN?

. . . YOU KNOW WHAT IT MEANS.

WHOA.
NICE HAIR.

YOU LOOK LIKE A LITTLE BOY OFF TO SHOOT A SQUIRREL FOR DINNER.

. . . YOU GONNA SHOOT AN ACTUAL TARGET TODAY?
NO.

I TOLD YOU, I'M WAITING FOR LIBBY.
COME **ON**!

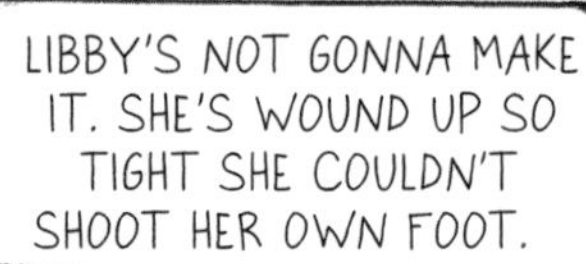
LIBBY'S NOT GONNA MAKE IT. SHE'S WOUND UP SO TIGHT SHE COULDN'T SHOOT HER OWN FOOT.

DO YOU REALLY WANT TO GO HOME WITH **ONE** TARGET LEFT?

AT LEAST SHOOT SOME PRACTICE BULLS. YOU DON'T HAVE TO SHOOT THE WHOLE THING. JUST TAKE A FEW SHOTS.

UGH, NICKY, FINE!
YES!
CLAP

OK, JUST SHOOT WHERE I TELL YOU. IT'LL BE LIKE A GAME!

BULL ONE.
GO.

BANG

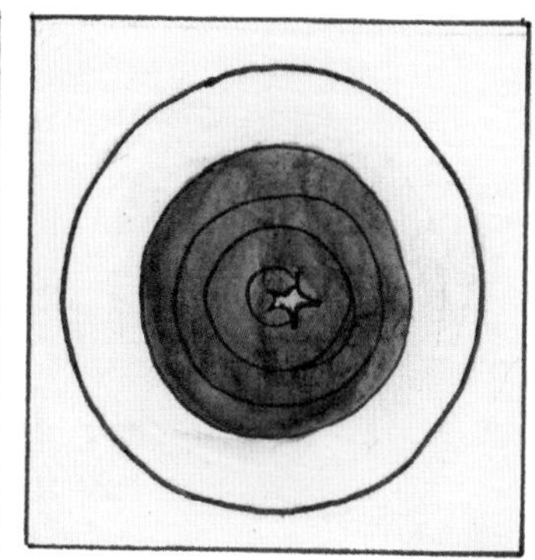

NICE SHOT, AGAIN.

BULL FOUR.
NOW BULL ONE.

PERFECT, AGAIN.

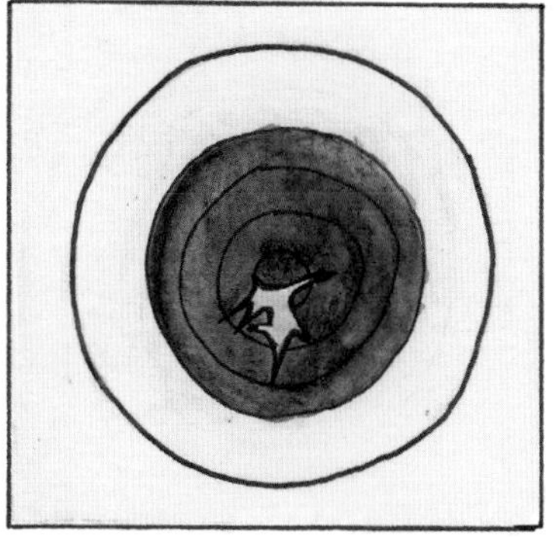

BULL FOUR.

BULL ONE.
BANG

GUESS WHAT?
. . . WHAT?

YOU JUST SHOT YOUR D.E.

WHAT?
WAIT.
I DIDN'T MEAN TO.
IT'S DONE. YOU CAN'T UNDO IT.
IF LIBBY FINDS OUT —
HEY Y'ALL! MAGGIE JUST SHOT IT DEAD!
NICKY, SHH!
ALISON, GO CALL IT ON THE LOUDSPEAKER.
NO
NO NO

ATTENTION Y'ALL. MAGGIE
THRASH JUST SHOT HER D.E.!
I THINK YOU'RE THE FIRST PERSON IN HISTORY TO ACCIDENTALLY SHOOT THEIR DISTINGUISHED EXPERT.

LIBBY'S GONNA BE SO MAD AT ME.
SORRY.

BUT YOU'RE A WINNER, MAGGIE. I COULDN'T JUST SIT HERE AND LET YOU THROW THAT AWAY.

MAGGIE!

CONGRA —

SMACK

BACK-STABBER!

UUUGH

WHOA.
WHAT IS WRONG WITH YOU?

WHY ARE YOU ALWAYS IN MY FACE?

YOU DON'T EVEN TAKE RIFLE!

STAY AWAY FROM ME OR I'LL KILL YOU!

JESUS, DON'T SAY THAT WITH GUNS AROUND!

WHAT'S GOING ON DOWN THERE?

COME ON, LET'S JUST GO.

CONGRATULATIONS ON BEING A DISTINGUISHED ASSHOLE!

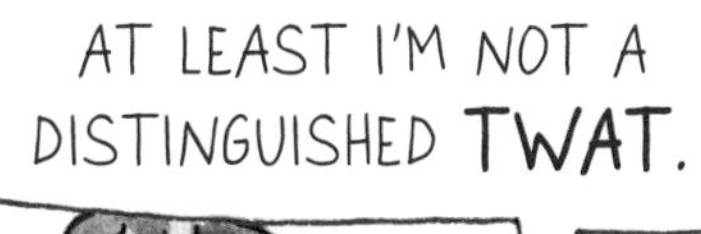
AT LEAST I'M NOT A DISTINGUISHED TWAT.

SNORT

DISTINGUISHED TWAT?

HA HA HA

HA HA HA

OH MY GOD, WHAT IS THAT GIRL'S PROBLEM?

SHE'S SUCH A VIOLENT FREAK.
THAT'S THE SECOND TIME SHE'S ATTACKED ME.

AND IT'S ALWAYS, LIKE, ON LIBBY'S BEHALF.
I WISH I HAD SUCH A WEIRDLY DEVOTED FRIEND.

I'M TOTALLY WEIRDLY DEVOTED.
PUNCH
IT JUST SHOWS IN A DIFFERENT WAY.

I MEAN, DO YOU REALLY NEED ME TO GO AROUND ATTACKING YOUR RIVALS?
NO.

EXACTLY. YOU JUST NEED SOMEONE TO CHILL WITH.

TO BE REAL WITH.

HEY, NICKY, IS MAGGIE HERE?
I THINK SHE RAN OFF.
DO YOU KNOW WHERE SHE WENT?
NO.
MAGGIE
IS THAT HER TARGET?
YEAH.
CAN I LOOK AT IT?
SURE.
IT'S PRETTY MUCH THE FLYEST BULL I'VE EVER SEEN.

I HEARD SHE'S BEEN CRYING ALL DAY.

ARE YOU GONNA APOLOGIZE TO HER?
NO. IT WAS AN ACCIDENT. NICKY TRICKED ME.

YOU REALIZE NO ONE BELIEVES THAT. . . .
SHRUG

HEY, WHAT DID ERIN THINK OF YOUR HAIR?
I DON'T KNOW. . . .

SHE'S BEEN AVOIDING ME.

WHADDA THEY GONNA DO? **SEND ME HOME?!**
HA HA HA
Sharnia

WELL, TONIGHT'S YOUR LAST CHANCE.
I HEARD SHE'S NOT COMING BACK NEXT YEAR.

HEARD FROM WHO?
I DUNNO. SOME JUNIORS.

I MEAN, SHE'S PRETTY OLD FOR THIS PLACE.

ATTENTION, LADIES. THERE ARE CANDLES HERE FOR EVERYONE.
CANDLES
CANDLES

WE'LL ALL WALK TOGETHER TO CAMPFIRE HILL, TO HONOR OUR BEST AND BRIGHTEST AT THE AWARDS CEREMONY.

The turn of the millennium was the height of "everyone's a winner" parenting. Most camps were dispensing with awards or else making sure everyone got one, so no one would feel left out or have low self-esteem. Not so with us; here we did things the old way. There were only a few awards, and only a few girls got them, and everyone else envied them bitterly.

DO YOU THINK YOU'LL GET SPIRIT OF RIFLE?
ME?
WHO ELSE?

USUALLY A SIXTEEN GETS THAT AWARD.
CUZ USUALLY A SIXTEEN'S THE BEST. BUT THIS YEAR YOU ARE.

For a second I actually felt optimistic. I mean, I **really** didn't want to go home. What was I going to do — tell my parents I liked girls now? I was supposed to be doing my pre-debutante cotillion that fall, and there was zero room to be gay in that crowd. But maybe if I got Spirit of Rifle, it would be a little better. . . . My dad loved guns. He had a whole closet full of them for bird hunting. And my mom loved displaying fancy things. Maybe that would be enough to distract them.

Friendliest Camper
Happiest Camper
Senior Camp Achievement

LOOK AT JENNY'S FACE.
SHE TOTALLY THOUGHT SHE WAS GETTING HAPPIEST CAMPER.

NOT SO HAPPY NOW. . . .

THIS NEXT AWARD GOES TO A GIRL WHO'S HAD SOME UPS AND DOWNS THIS SUMMER.
THIS SHOULD BE A PRETTY BIG UP.

I hoped Erin was watching. Because once I got that silver cup, I wouldn't just be some barely-fifteen-year-old camper she randomly met. I'd be the Spirit of Rifle, and then no one could shame her for liking me.

SPIRIT OF RIFLE IS LIBBY MULLIGAN.
WOW, THAT'S A CRIME.
I don't know why I was so mad. It hadn't even occurred to me that I could get Spirit of Rifle before Bethany mentioned it. But it was amazing how quickly I'd come to see that award as **mine.** And amazing how quickly it was taken away.
NOW FOR OUR SPECIAL AWARD. THE ONE WE GIVE TO THE GIRL WHO EMBODIED OUR SPECIAL SPIRIT.

. . . DID SHE JUST SAY YOUR NAME?
HM?
OH MY GOD.
HOLD OUT YOUR CANDLE.
DO IT!
YOU'RE HONOR GIRL!

I kept expecting someone to tell me to sit down. Maybe Shannon had misheard my name or was messing with me. But the Honor Girls of summers past were just staring at me with their creepy, affectionate smiles. They were the prettiest, nicest girls in camp. The kind who went around comforting homesick juniors and organizing sing-alongs. I had no idea what I was doing with them.

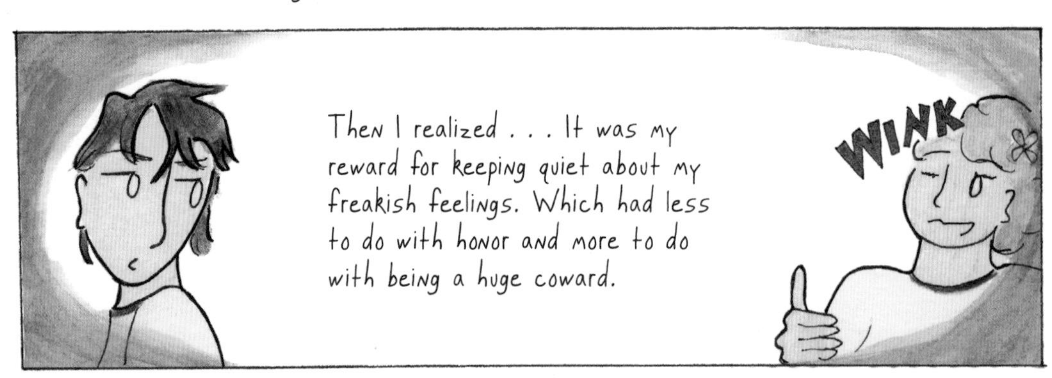

Then I realized . . . It was my reward for keeping quiet about my freakish feelings. Which had less to do with honor and more to do with being a huge coward.
WINK

Maybe I should have felt victorious, but instead I just felt embarrassed and kind of appalled — that a sham this big was on **me.**

YOU'RE AN HONOR GIRL NOW AND FOREVER.
SIGN THE BOOK.
IT'S FULL OF MESSAGES FROM EVERY HONOR GIRL SINCE 1922.
I CAN'T WAIT TO READ WHAT BEING AN HONOR GIRL MEANS TO YOU.
SO SO SO SO SO SO SO SO SO SO SO SO SO SO SO SO SO SO HAPPY!
honor girl forever! –jenny o'neal
always fills my soul
1923
I love you
Sarah Hart 1979
I will carry this in my heart for the rest of my life
1953
~Karen Kay
can't believe this
never been so happ
entire life!!!!!
Peyton Price
SUCH A SURPRISE,
TEARS RUNNING
JUST WANT TO SAY
HOW FULL OF LOVE
fun
laughter, love
friendship, leadership
tradition, a place where I can truly be myself
Jackie
1981
the most
special plac

This is the Book of Frauds because I shouldn't even be here and everyone is so fake it makes me want to go on a killing spree.
HONOR GIRL IS THE STUPIDEST FUCKING THING I'VE EVER HEARD

I don't know what to say because I didn't expect to be part of this camp history forever. I don't feel great about this. I feel really weird. But I'm gonna sign this book now. I guess if you're reading this it means you're Honor Girl too, so congrats. I hope it means something?

-Maggie Thrash, 2000

P.S. I just realized I'm the first Honor Girl of the entire millennium. Jesus Christ, this camp will probably outlast us all.

MAGGIE!
. . . YES?
ERIN'S PLAYING GUITAR FOR THE JUNIORS.
I CAN HEAR IT FROM MY TENT!
COME ON!

WAIT, I DON'T WANT HER TO SEE ME.
PUSH

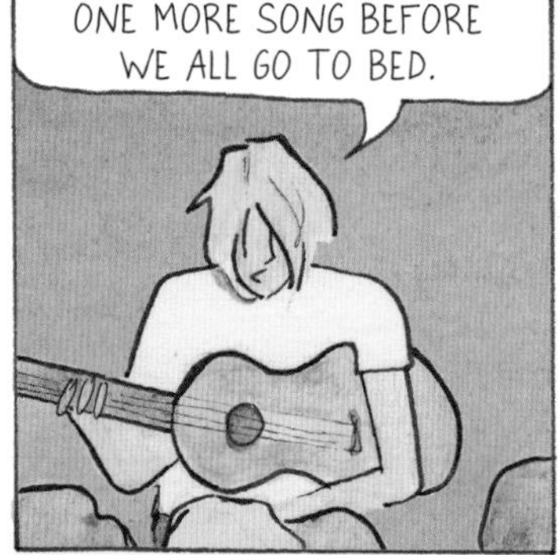
ONE MORE SONG BEFORE WE ALL GO TO BED.

THIS ONE'S A LUUUUUUV SONG.

OOOOOOOOOOOHHHH

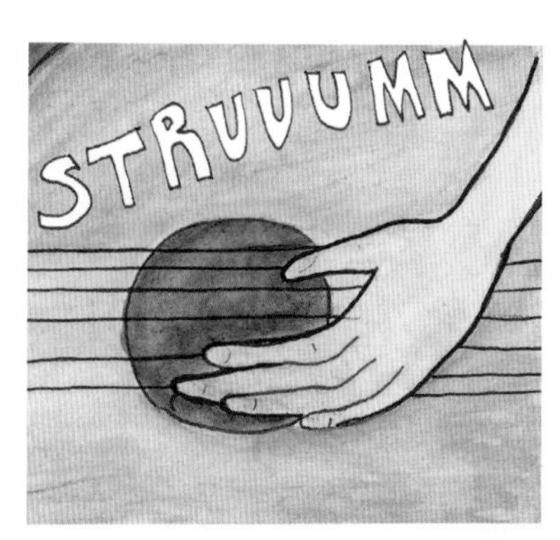
STRUUUMM

LOOKING IN YOUR EYES,

YOU PUT UP NO DISGUISE,

BUT EVERYTHING YOU DO . . .

IS LIKE A MYSTERY

. . .

YOU ARE AN UNTOUCHABLE ANGEL.

OH MY GOD.

IT'S ABOUT **YOU**!
SHUT UP, BETHANY.

SHE CAN'T **TOUCH** YOU!
'CUZ YOU'RE A **CAMPER**!
SHUT **UP**!

. . . I WISH I COULD TELL YOU THAT . . .

I THINK YOU'RE WONDERFUL

BUT SOMETHING STOPS ME AND NERVOUSLY I FLEE . . .

WHILE THE MEMORY OF YOUR FACE . . . IT BURNS IN MY MIND.

IT **BURNS** HER **MIND**, MAGGIE!
SHAKE

YOU ARE MY UNTOUCHABLE ANGEL
BUT COURAGE TAKES ITS TIME . . .

OH. MY. GOD. WHAT ARE YOU GONNA DO?
DO?

YOU HAVE TO, LIKE, GO TO HER!
GO TO HER, THRASH!

I'M NOT GONNA "GO TO HER" WITH FIVE BILLION CHILDREN AROUND.
THE SONG'S PROBABLY NOT EVEN ABOUT ME.

IT'S PROBABLY ABOUT . . . A DOG.
A DOG? AN UNTOUCHABLE DOG?

YEAH, LIKE, IT ROLLED AROUND IN GARBAGE, SO IT'S ALL FILTHY.
ARE YOU SERIOUS?

MAGGIE, YOU'RE LETTING THIS MOMENT DISAPPEAR.
IT'S DISAPPEARING AS WE SPEAK!
THEN JUST LET IT, BETHANY!

NOT EVERY MOMENT HAS TO HAPPEN.

IF I LOVED SOMEONE, I WOULDN'T JUST WALK AWAY FROM THEM.
IF I LOVED SOMEONE, I WOULDN'T RUIN IT BY ACTING PREMATURELY.
IT IS **NOT** IMMATURE TO BE TRUE TO YOUR FEELINGS.
I SAID **PRE**MATURE, NOT **IM**MATURE.
OH . . .
IT'S THE **LAST** NIGHT, MAGGIE!
THAT'S NOT ENOUGH OF A REASON.
It was possible that after tonight I would never see her again. But that fact didn't feel motivating, just overwhelming. It was too much to ask that I carry this weird amorphous love on my own. Maybe the song was about me. But what did that matter if she hadn't meant for me to hear it?

CHAPTER 12
Good-byes

Our good-byes were never very heartfelt. The last morning was so aggravating — trying to get your stuff together, other people's parents everywhere — you didn't feel like crying or getting emotional about it. I was always one of the last to leave, since my mom had farther to drive. The counselors would start taking down tents, like they couldn't even wait till we were gone.

YOUR FACE! IT BURNS MY MIND!
HILARIOUS.

HERE'S MY ADDRESS. WRITE AND TELL ME WHAT HAPPENS WITH E-R-I-N.
IT'LL PROBABLY BE A BLANK PAGE OF NOTHING.

SEE YOU NEXT YEAR!
BYE . . .

SO . . .
SO . . .

THAT WAS KIND OF A WEIRD SUMMER.
YEP.

I MEAN, NOT LIKE, CATACLYSMICALLY WEIRD. JUST . . . IRREGULAR.

YOU'RE A POET, SHANNON.
SLAP

TILL NEXT YEAR . . .

I hope you are having a fun summer while I languish in this sanatorium for the deformed. Despite the acute and ongoing pain of having my sternum LITERALLY RECONSTRUCTED, I definitely definitely care about your problems, i.e., emerging gynephilia. Just kidding, I don't. But if I did, I would say that given the scenario you proposed, the odds are very low:

$$\frac{4^2}{(2^2 \times 2^2 \times 2^2 \times 2^2) - 4^2} = \frac{16}{240} = \frac{1}{15}$$

However, you neglected to specify whether lower odds correlate to a higher degree of innate/manifest Sapphism or the inverse. So I am unable to draw a firm conclusion. Additionally I fail to see how this proposition relates in any way to sexual preferences.

bye

Drew

WHATCHA READIN'?

HEY!
IT'S FROM MY BROTHER.

I JUST GOT IT TWO SECONDS AGO.

HEY, CONGRATS ON HONOR GIRL.
THANKS . . .

I DON'T REALLY KNOW WHY I GOT IT . . .
I DO.

. . .

BECAUSE YOU WERE SO GREAT WITH LEXI WHEN SHE SPRAINED HER KNEE, HELPING HER GET AROUND AND STUFF.
OH . . .

I THINK THAT'S MY MOM.

LISTEN, I HAVE TO GO DO SOMETHING.
RIGHT NOW?

BUT I'LL BE RIGHT BACK.
TO SAY GOOD-BYE.
OK . . .

HELLOOOOO, PUDDLE DUCK!

GOOD LORD, WHAT HAVE YOU DONE TO YOURSELF?
SHRUG
WELL I WISH YOU'D ASKED ME FIRST.
I WOULD HAVE TOLD YOU YOUR NOSE IS TOO BIG FOR THAT HAIRSTYLE!

twenty minutes later
WE REALLY NEED TO GO, SWEETHEART.
WE HAVE TICKETS FOR *BRIGADOON*!

MY FRIEND SAID SHE WAS COMING BACK . . .
I'M SURE SHE MEANT **NEXT SUMMER.**

COME ON, NOW.
THE BARGE WON'T WAIT FOREVER.

GOOD-BYE, MINNIE.

I think I knew the whole time that she wasn't coming back.

FIGHTING BISHOP INN,
KNOXVILLE, TN
KNOCK
KNOCK

YOU'RE NOT WEARING **THAT**? WHAT ABOUT YOUR LILLY PULITZER?

UM, THAT'S NOT REALLY MY STYLE ANYMORE. . . .

OF COURSE IT IS! LILLY PULITZER IS THE VERY ESSENCE OF STYLE.

TOSS

THE POPLAR
THEATER PRESENTS
BRIGADOON

Brigadoon is a musical about an enchanted village in Scotland that appears once every 100 years.

Then one day an American tourist stumbles upon it.

THIS WASN'T ON THE MAP. . . .

He falls in love with a bonnie lassie and decides to stay in Brigadoon forever.

But he can't because the enchantment breaks and Brigadoon disappears into the mist.

FIONA!
FIONA!

BRIGADOON, BRIGADOON,
there my heart forever lies.

CHAPTER 13
Civilization

MONTHS LATER, IN ATLANTA

I didn't bother telling my parents. It's not like I had an actual girlfriend or any immediate reason to upset the family universe. Except I was so depressed, I hadn't done any homework or taken a shower in a month.

MAGGIE WISHED SHE COULD COME, BUT SHE'S HAVING HER RETAINER TIGHTENED.
ORTHODONTIA IS SO IMPORTANT FOR SELF-ESTEEM.

When my mom finally noticed, she said she refused to be seen with me in public until I washed my hair. Which was fine with me because I didn't feel like going to church or pre-debutante cotillion luncheons or the mall anyway. My mom got pretty good at making excuses.

Both times I tried telling someone that I was possibly gay now, it ended with them insisting to me that I wasn't. The first was my best friend since 6th grade. The second was my gym teacher.

It was basically the same speech she gave to girls who tried to get out of sit-ups because they were on their periods.

I sent Erin three letters addressed to the University of Colorado.

I didn't know if she never got them or just never replied.

After a few months I gave up wondering either way.

I spent most of that year in the basement with my brother watching *Babylon 5*. I got really obsessed with it, partly because of this maddening hint that Lieutenant Ivanova was a lesbian.

When no one was around, I'd sit on the roof of the house and shoot acorns with my dad's .22. You could do that sort of thing in Georgia without anyone calling the police.

It wasn't about staying sharp. It was about feeling that feeling again — aim, fire, unload — of being totally focused yet totally blank. And the ringing in your ears that stayed with you long after you pulled the trigger.

I shouldn't have gone back the next summer, but I did. If there was the slightest chance that she would be there, I had to be there too.

She wasn't.

Everything was the same. That shouldn't have surprised me — wasn't it always the same? But it seemed unbelievable this time that things could just go on, oblivious of me, with no sympathy for the fact that I was a different person now.

It turns out that once you have your D.E., there's not much left to do. I started shooting random stuff, but after a while, that started to feel pointless. What was the point of being that good? It's not like I was a hunter or an assassin.

I was just a girl with a weirdly deadly toy.

AFTERWORD
Puye Cliffs,
17 years old

SHOULD WE GO IN?

BAH!
AHHHHH!

HA HA HA HA

WHERE DID HE GET THAT GIANT LOLLIPOP?
IS THERE A CARNIVAL NEARBY?

OH, YOU CAN GET THOSE AT WALMART NOWADAYS.
REALLY? I'VE NEVER BEEN TO WALMART.

WHAT?
SHRUG

MY MOM SAYS WALMART IS TRASHY.
WELL, YEAH, IT'S TOTALLY TRASHY.

AND I'M TOTALLY TAKING YOU THERE.
COME ON.
WAIT, NOW?

SURE, THIS PLACE ISN'T GOING ANYWHERE.

IT'S BEEN HERE A THOUSAND YEARS.

HEY, WHY WAS YOUR PHONE NUMBER SO HARD TO FIND?
IT WAS LIKE THE THRASHES DIDN'T EXIST.
WE'RE UNLISTED 'CUZ MY DAD'S A JUDGE. . . .

I GUESS THEY DON'T WANT CRIMINALS CALLING THE HOUSE.
RIGHT . . .

SO YOU'RE A SENIOR? HAVE YOU PICKED OUT COLLEGES?

NOT REALLY. MY SAT SCORES ARE ABYSMAL, WHICH LIMITS THINGS. . . .

It was hard to know what to talk about. What had we talked about at camp? I couldn't even remember. Obviously not my SAT scores. At camp no one talked about stuff like that, like we'd all unconsciously agreed to leave those things behind.

And now, instinctively I guess, Erin and I were doing the opposite. Leaving camp behind, not talking about it, maybe so it would feel less foreign and weird to be stranded outside it.

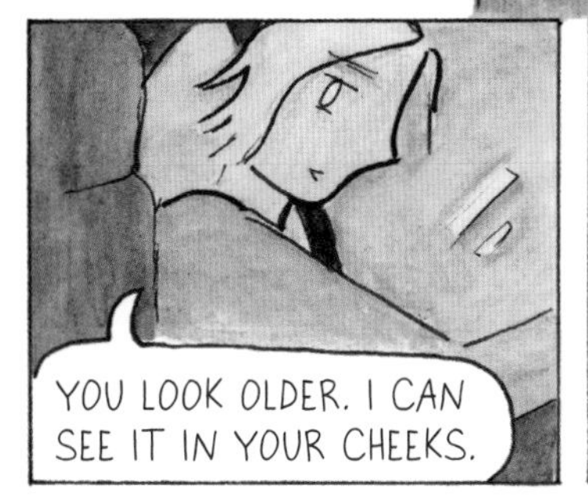

YOU LOOK OLDER. I CAN SEE IT IN YOUR CHEEKS.

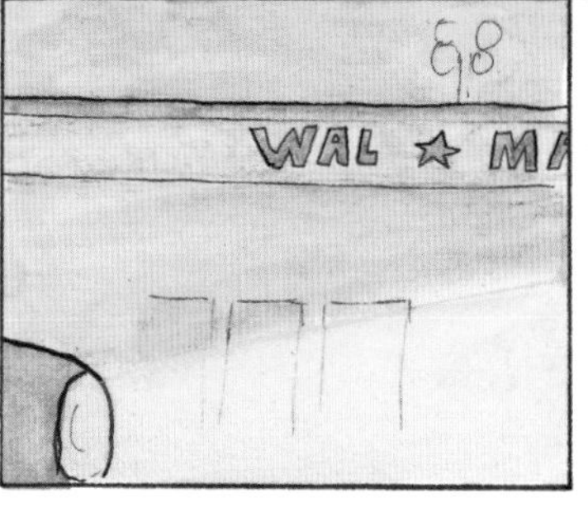

. . . YOU LOOK THE SAME.

lemon
RUSH

Dr
POP

ULTRA
VANILLA
TIME

Fizzz

LOOK, THEY HAVE EVERY KIND OF SODA.
EVERYDAY $ VALUES

NO, YOU GOTTA GET THE BIG CUP. THE 60-OUNCE.

MAKE IT A SUICIDE.
GULP

WHOA. IT'S HEAVY!
I WANNA SEE YOU DRINK THE WHOLE THING.

WHAT? THAT'S NOT A SUICIDE, THAT'S AN AMICICIDE.

WHAT DOES THAT MEAN?

AMICICIDE. IT'S, UM, THE KILLING OF A FRIEND.

Magic Blast

Popsi

cherry Smooth CRASH

GUZZLE

. . . DID YOU GET MY LETTERS?
LETTERS? NO.
FUTON $199

DO YOU NOT BELIEVE ME?
SHRUG

I THOUGHT ABOUT YOU. A LOT.

ACTUALLY I WROTE A SONG ABOUT YOU A FEW MONTHS AGO. . . .

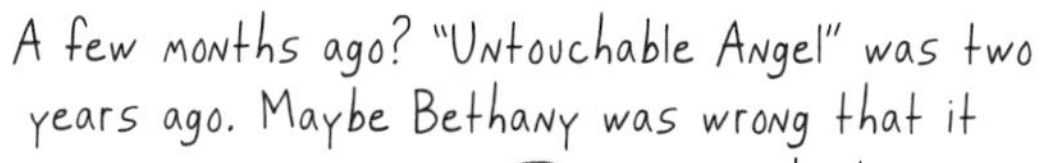
A few months ago? "Untouchable Angel" was two years ago. Maybe Bethany was wrong that it was about me.

WHAT'S IT CALLED?

WAIT. NEVER MIND, DON'T TELL ME. IT'LL MAKE ME FEEL SELF-CONSCIOUS.

OH, DON'T WORRY. THE TITLE IS VERY VAGUE AND REVEALS NOTHING.
"BROWN HAIR PERSON FEELINGS MELODY."

ARE YOU OK?
YOU SEEM . . . TIGHTLY WOUND.
GAHH!
WHOA.
OH MY GOD.
SORRY.
I'M JUST . . . I'M TRYING TO ACT NORMAL, BUT I'M A TAD . . . OVERWHELMED.
IT'S OK . . . WALMART CAN HAVE THAT EFFECT.
SO CAN A THOUSAND GRAMS OF SUGAR.

HERE, GIVE ME THAT. LET'S GET OUT OF HERE. WE CAN GO TO THE PLACE WHERE I'M STAYING.

IT'S A SQUALID LITTLE ADOBE SHIT-SHACK.
SOUNDS CHARMING.
TRASH

EVERYDAY $ VALUES

DESERT ROSE
MOTEL

HOW LONG WAS THE DRIVE HERE FROM BOULDER?
NOT BAD. SEVEN HOURS.

SEVEN HOURS?

MAYBE THAT SEEMS FAR TO YOU. . . . OUT HERE, EVERYTHING'S FAR APART.

WHOA. YOU STILL HAVE THIS?

YEAH . . . BUT IT'S FALLING APART.

WOW, THIS LOOKS HARD.

How big would a spherical asteroid have to be thrown at 100 mph to escape? The asteroid is 3000 kgm.

$v_{esc} = 100 \frac{miles}{hour} \times 1\ hour$

$density = 300 \frac{kg}{m^3}$

$v_{esc} = \sqrt{\frac{2Gm}{R}}$ (Eq 6.5)

$density = \frac{mass}{4 \cdot \pi r^3}$ (Eq 6.7)

I ALWAYS READ THAT TO MY STUDENTS AND TELL THEM, IF YOU'RE HERE BECAUSE YOU THINK STARS ARE PRETTY AND TELESCOPES ARE COOL, THEN YOU'RE IN FOR A GRUELING REALITY CHECK. . . .

. . . I MEAN, STARS ARE PRETTY, YEAH, BUT WHAT DO THEY **DO**? WHAT DO THEY **MEAN**? WITHOUT MATH THEY'RE JUST . . . FARAWAY SPARKLY THINGS THAT SHOW UP AT NIGHT.
DESERT ROSE MOTEL

I'M TERRIBLE AT MATH. I GUESS I'LL NEVER KNOW WHAT THE STARS MEAN.

WELL, I'M EXCELLENT AT MATH, SO . . .
I CAN JUST TELL YOU.

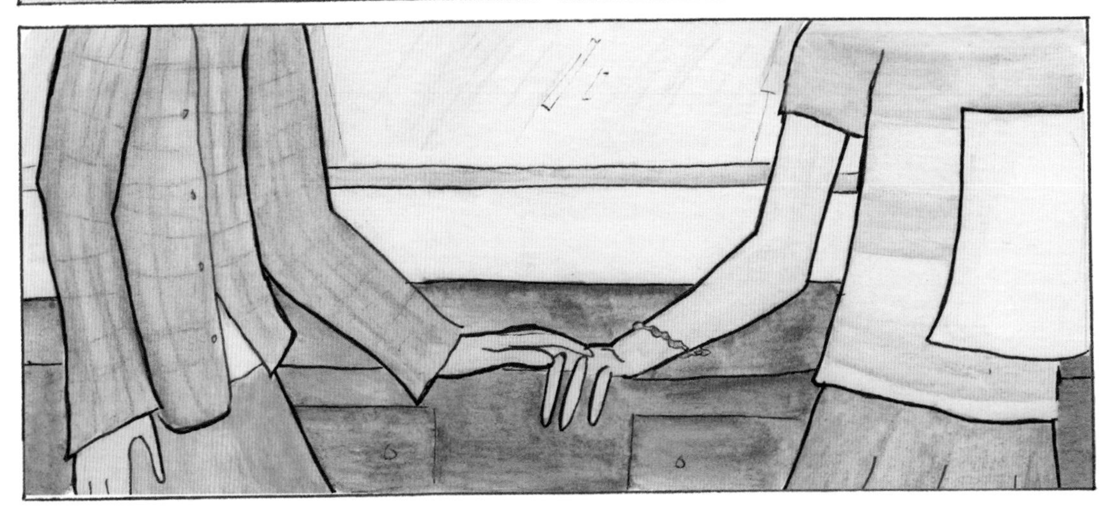

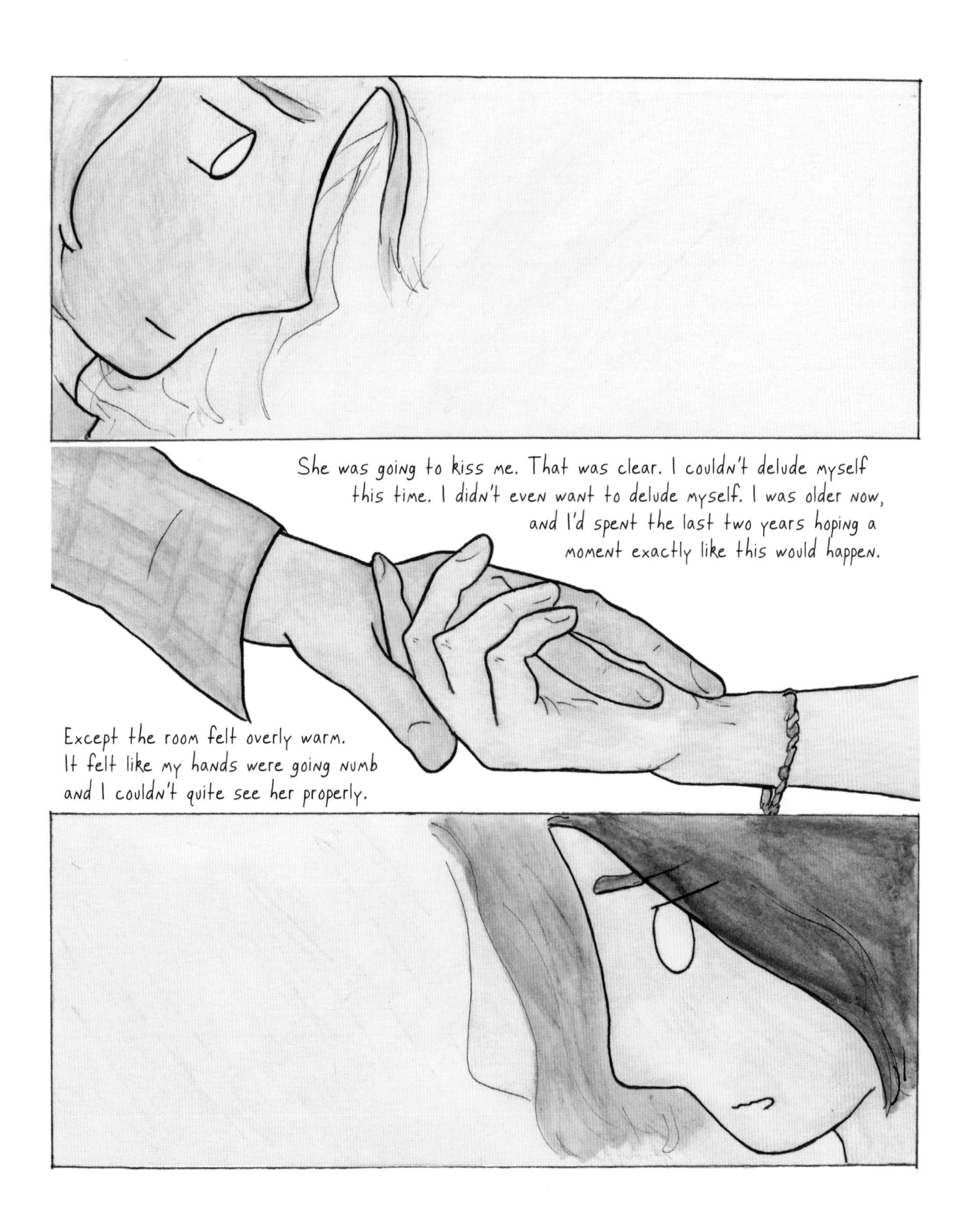
She was going to kiss me. That was clear. I couldn't delude myself this time. I didn't even want to delude myself. I was older now, and I'd spent the last two years hoping a moment exactly like this would happen.
Except the room felt overly warm. It felt like my hands were going numb and I couldn't quite see her properly.

MAGGIE.

OH MY GOD.

ARE YOU OK? SHOULD I CALL YOUR MOM?

NO.

I MEAN . . . I'M FINE. CAN I JUST USE YOUR BATHROOM?
SURE . . .

FIX IT.

I TOLD YOU THAT SUICIDE WOULD KILL ME!

HA.

ARE WE GOING SOMEWHERE?

I SHOULD TAKE YOU BACK TO YOUR HOTEL.

WAIT, WHAT?
I SWEAR I'M FINE. IT WAS JUST TOO MUCH SUGAR. . . .

Something had changed. She was wary of me now, I could tell. Like she'd realized I wasn't as mature or self-possessed as I'd seemed. That this was way too big of a deal to me. She was smiling, but in a big-sisterly way that made me wish I'd stayed unconscious.

WE FORGOT TO LOOK FOR THE LOLLIPOP.

HM?

AT WALMART.

OH, THAT . . . THEY MIGHT NOT HAVE HAD IT ANYWAY.

IT WAS GREAT TO SEE YOU, MAGGIE. I ALWAYS FELT TERRIBLE THAT WE NEVER SAID GOOD-BYE.
YOU KNOW . . . THAT LAST DAY.

It seemed weird that she said "we." As if it had been a fluke or a mutual error.

I didn't say anything. Why did it always feel like this love was up to me?

COME HERE.
It wasn't a good hug. Our arms sort of knocked together, and then she pulled away from me. She didn't even take off her seat belt.

SLAM

DOUBLE WHISKEY?

SURE.

HA. TRY A SHIRLEY TEMPLE.

SWING

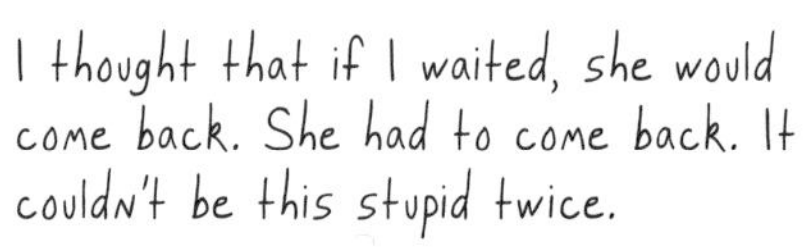
I thought that if I waited, she would come back. She had to come back. It couldn't be this stupid twice.

THAT'S A SWEET DRINK FOR SUCH A SOUR FACE.

DON'T

DIN MEAN NUTHIN.

I stayed there for as long as I could. For as long as I could convince myself she might come back. Then, at a certain point, it was just clear. . . .
What am I doing here? It's over.

it's over, it's

over, it's over

This is a work of nonfiction. The events and experiences detailed herein have been described from the author's memory. Some names, identities, and circumstances have been changed to protect the privacy and/or anonymity of the various individuals involved.

Maggie Thrash attended Hampshire College and the Sewanee University of the South. She hasn't shot a gun in ten years.

All my gratitude to Stephen Barr, whose idea this was.

Thank you to the universal mind at Candlewick, particularly my editor Katie Cunningham, Liz Bickwell, Laila Milevski, Sherry Fatla, and Gregg Hammerquist.

Special thanks to my BFF Nico. I'm pretty sure everyone thinks he's imaginary, but he's real and I couldn't have made this without him.

Copyright Acknowledgments

First edition 2015

Library of Congress Catalog Card Number 2014951805
ISBN 978-0-7636-7382-6

15 16 17 18 19 20 CCP 10 9 8 7 6 5 4 3 2 1

Printed in Shenzhen, Guangdong, China

This book was typeset in Maggie Thrash.
The illustrations were done in watercolor pencil and pen, and completed digitally.

Candlewick Press
99 Dover Street
Somerville, Massachusetts 02144

visit us at www.candlewick.com